152 Ways to Keep Students in School

Effective, Easy-to-Implement Tips for Teachers

Franklin P. Schargel

EYE ON EDUCATION
6 DEPOT WAY WEST, SUITE 106
LARCHMONT, NY 10538
(914) 833–0551
(914) 833–0761 fax
www.eyeoneducation.com

Schargel, Franklin P.
152 ways to keep students in school: effective, easy-to-implement tips for teachers / by Franklin Schargel.

p. cm.
ISBN 978-1-59667-087-7
1. Dropouts—United States—Prevention. 2. Motivation in education—United States. 3. Teachers—In-service training—United States.
I. Title. II. Title: One hundred fifty two ways to keep students in school.
LC143.S219 2008
371.2'913—dc22   2008009987

10 9 8 7 6 5 4 3 2 1

Editorial and production services provided by
Hypertext Book and Journal Services
738 Saltillo St., San Antonio, TX 78207-6953 (210-227-6055)

Also Available from EYE ON EDUCATION

From At Risk to Academic Excellence:
What Successful Leaders Do
Franklin P. Schargel, Tony Thacker, John S. Bell

Best Practices to Help At-Risk Learners
Franklin P. Schargel

Helping Students Graduate
Jay Smink and Franklin P. Schargel

Dropout Prevention Tools
Franklin P. Schargel

Strategies to Help Solve Our School Dropout Problem
Franklin P. Schargel and Jay Smink

Classroom Motivation from A to Z:
How to Engage Your Students in Learning
Barbara R. Blackburn

Teach Me—I Dare You
Judith Brough, Sherrel Bergmann, and Larry Holt

How to Reach and Teach All Students: Simplified!
Elizabeth Breaux

Teach My Kid—I Dare You!
The Educator's Essential Guide to Parent Involvement
Bergmann, Brough and Shepard

101 "Answers" for New Teachers and Their Mentors:
Effective Teaching Tips for Daily Classroom Use
Annette L. Breaux

Classroom Instruction from A to Z:
How to Promote Student Learning
Barbara R. Blackburn

Handbook on Differentiated Instruction
for Middle and High Schools
Sheryn Spencer Northey

At-Risk Students:
Reaching and Teaching Them, Second Edition
Richard Sagor and Jonas Cox

High-Impact Leadership for High-Impact Schools:
The Actions That Matter Most
Pamela Salazar

What Great Teachers Do *Differently*:
14 Things That Matter Most
Todd Whitaker

What Great Principals Do *Differently*:
15 Things That Matter Most
Todd Whitaker

What Successful Principals Do!
169 Tips for Principals
Franzy Fleck

Improving Your School One Week At a Time:
Building the Foundation for Professional Teaching & Learning
Jeffrey Zoul

Lead With Me:
A Principal's Guide to Teacher Leadership
Gayle Moller and Anita Pankake

The Instructional Leader's Guide to
Informal Classroom Observations
Sally J. Zepeda

Lead Me—I Dare You!
Sherrel Bergman and Judith Brough

BRAVO Principal!
Sandra Harris

The Administrator's Guide to
School Community Relations, 2nd Edition
George E. Pawlas

The Principal as Instructional Leader:
A Handbook for Supervisors, 2nd Edition
Sally J. Zepeda

Acknowledgments

There are so many people who need to be acknowledged and thanked.

First, my family, Sandra my wife, my favorite critic, who is insightful, demonstrates wisdom, inspires, and provides guidance. To my children, David, Howard, and Pegi for their insights and for helping to keep my feet firmly placed on terra firma. To my sister, Eleanor and brother, Eddie —thank you for being there when I need you.

To the people at Eye On Education: To Dan, Michelle, Heather, Kate, and Jennifer, you make my life so much easier. Thank you for being there. To my publisher, Bob Sickles, who when he heard my vision of this book, encouraged me, provided vision, and always was accessible

To the educators in the field: You face far greater challenges and shoulder far larger burdens now than you endured with my generation. I appreciate your dedication and love of children. We know that you do it in spite of poor working conditions and low pay. We are all lost without you.

Albuquerque, NM 2008

In Memory

John Phillip Siskind
March 21, 1944–Nov. 19, 2007

Colleague
Visionary
Friend

Table of Contents

Meet the Author

Franklin Schargel, a native of Brooklyn now residing in Albuquerque, New Mexico, is a graduate of the University of the City of New York. Franklin holds a master's degree in secondary education from City University and another in school administration and supervision from Pace University. His career spans 33 years of classroom teaching and counseling and 8 years of supervision and administration as an assistant principal. In addition, Franklin taught a course in Dowling College's MBA program.

Franklin served on the Guidelines Development Committee for the Malcolm Baldrige National Quality Award in Education and was for 2 years an examiner for the Baldrige Award. In addition, he served as a judge for the Secretary of the Air Force Quality Award and a judge for the USA Today/RIT Quality Cup. He recently completed his term as chair of the American Society of Quality's Education Division.

As senior managing associate of his training firm, School Success Network, Franklin has presented countless workshops for educational, community, and business groups throughout the United States, Europe, Canada, and Latin America. His workshops are for administrators, teachers, students, parents, business leaders, policymakers, and anyone else interested in building world-class schools. The workshops cover a wide variety of topics, including dealing with at-risk school populations, dropout prevention, consensus building, curriculum innovation, educational leadership, empowerment of staff, interactive learning, the Malcolm Baldrige National Quality Award in Education, organizational change, parental involvement, problem solving, career and technical education, strategic planning, student evaluation and data analysis, teamwork, tech prep, and total quality education. All his workshops are tailored to the individual client's needs and expected outcomes.

He is the author of six well-received books: *From At Risk to Academic Excellence: What Successful Leaders Do; Strategies to Help Solve Our School Dropout Problem; Dropout Prevention Tools; Helping Students Graduate; Best Practices to Help At-Risk Learners*, and *Transforming Education Through Total Quality Management: A Practitioner's Guide*, as well as more than 65 articles published in leading educational journals and business magazines. Mr. Schargel has a regular monthly Internet column at www.guidancechannel.com.

Franklin's success in dramatically enhancing the learning process in his inner-city school, expanding parental involvement, increasing postsecondary school attendance, and significantly lowering the students' dropout rate has been well documented in 25 books, 55 newspaper and magazine articles (including *Business Week, Fortune,* and the *New York Times*), and five internationally released videos (including a Public Broadcasting special).

In 2005, Mr. Schargel received the Crystal Star Award from the National Dropout Prevention Center.

Introduction

Of the seven books I have been in involved in, this was the easiest and hardest to write—easiest, because I've lived it; hardest, because it is so personal. I was a classroom teacher in six schools, a counselor in one, and a school administrator in three.

Over the years we in education gain personal insights and experience "aha" moments. I have successfully applied what you will read in the following pages, as have people I've supervised, and others whose workshops I have attended. They work. They have been field tested by professionals like you. Hopefully, they can help you as they've helped me and the students I have worked with. Ideally you can use all of them. Perhaps you can use most of them. Hopefully, they will turn a light on for you and you can add them to your repertoire of tools you use in the classroom.

We are no longer dealing exclusively with traditional students who come from traditional families. The traditional student focuses on the value of education, as does their family. Women served as stay-at-home mothers insuring that when a child came home the first thing they did was homework. Parents see education as a way up in American society. Traditional parents believe that education will not only aid the child but the family as well in terms of financial rewards but also as a prestige value in society.

But times have changed. Many of our students are not living in nuclear homes. They are being raised by aunts or grandparents, in foster homes, in merged families, or even homeless. We have children who are raising themselves and some are raising their own children. We have children who are coming from single-parent or two working-parent families. Stay-at-home mothers no longer dominate the American landscape. The U.S. Department of Labor estimates that two out of every three women with children under the age of 5 are in the workforce. This places an added burden on the school. Children are increasingly fed in schools and many of the traditional jobs of parents are now being placed in the school. School children sometimes have to stay at home with their younger siblings when their younger brothers or sisters are ill. Some parents feel it is the oldest child's responsibility to bring additional income into the home and therefore the oldest child needs to forgo high school graduation.

The job of teachers has become increasingly difficult and complex. This requires a different mindset and skillset from educators. Traditional teaching and learning techniques do not work with nontraditional students. If we wish to succeed with nontraditional students, as well as traditional students, we need to change what we teach—as well as how we teach them.

While I believe all applications must be rooted in theory, this book is all about application—the "how to do something" as opposed to the "why to do something."

For theory and application, I suggest that your read my other books, *Strategies to Help Solve Our School Dropout Problem*; *Helping Students Graduate: A Strategic Plan to End Dropouts*; and *From At-Risk to Academic Excellence: What Successful Leaders Do*, all published by Eye On Education.

This book also differs from my previous application books, *Dropout Prevention Tools* and *Best Practices to Help At-Risk Learners*, in that this book has short, punchy applications that I have used in my classroom, counseling office, or my role as an assistant principal. While I spent all my professional life in an urban high school, these instruments can be used in rural and suburban elementary, middle, as well as high schools.

The book is divided into four sections:

♦ Student Learning;
♦ Professional Growth;

- ♦ Family and Community Involvement; and
- ♦ Safe Schools.

The book was organized this way to facilitate reading, but I found that it was extremely difficult to categorize the items. Readers will realize that there are many overlaps. What may appear in Student Learning will bleed into Professional Growth, and so forth. The largest section is the one dealing with Student Learning since I feel it is the primary reason why this book has been written.

The suggestions I am making can be and have been used in all grades with all types of students. They were designed and written to be read quickly and easily implemented. They were designed to be concise snapshots of what educators can do to keep students from dropping out.

The book was not designed as an end-all book. It is a work in progress. You, the reader, have many such practical ideas that you use. I would love to hear about what works for you. In the next edition of the book, if we choose your entry for publication, we will give you credit for your work.

Looking forward to hearing from you.

Franklin P. Schargel
Albuquerque, NM
www.schargel.com
franklin@schargel.com

Student Learning

The key to school success is student learning. It is the primary reason why schools exist. Traditionally, we have focused our attention on schools as teaching organizations. Peter Senge in his book, *The Fifth Discipline* talks about schools becoming learning organizations—not only student learning, but adult learning as well. High-stakes state testing programs and the NCLB legislation have focused a laserlike beam on student learning.

1 **Teach Your Children to Love Reading.** Educators believe that children love to read and children do not. Yet they have a hard time explaining the success of the *Harry Potter* series. Children, like adults, like to read what they like to read.

Who among us has read their computer-operating manual? Or the instructions for their 1040 income-tax form? We, like children, like to read what we like to read. Children *do* like to read. How else can you explain the *Harry Potter* phenomenon?

I can remember the short story that turned me on to reading. It was Frank Stockton's "The Lady or the Tiger"? Can you remember what short story, novel, or nonfiction book made this kind of impression on you? Why not explain to students your favorite book or short story, or author?

What one book, which you can obtain for free, do ALL students want to read? It's the instruction manual needed to get a driver's license. Maybe we should teach reading to reluctant readers using this book. In addition, driver's manuals also have an assessment that measures comprehension. My math and science teacher friends tell me that there are math and physics concepts that can be used in the driver's manual. Teachers can also use the foreign language version translated by ELL students into English.

Teachers can put copies of the instruction manual in the back of the classroom along with old copies of *Car and Driver*, *Sport's Illustrated*, *Glamour*, *Teen*, *People*, *US*, and *Seventeen*. Old copies of these magazines can be obtained from the school library or the public library. In addition, newsstands return the covers of these magazines for credit, to the publisher and generally throw out the rest.

Write a letter to the publishers and ask if you can obtain previous copies. In the letter explain the purpose of your request and tell them they have the ability to build new readership. Encourage the parents of your students to contribute to your library of magazines.

Use these magazines as an incentive to come early to your classroom. Make rules about when students can read them. For example, after they have finished taking a test.

2 | **Teach Students the Value of Planning.** Do you remember when we went to school and how, occasionally, we had to cram for a test or to cram when we needed to complete a paper? Students have always crammed. While some students need to have the pressure of an immediate deadline imposed on them, others suffer under that pressure. We may need to inform students and parents of the difficulties some students face. We can help students by suggesting that they begin studying, if possible, a little at a time, 1 week in advance of a test. This would mean that we have to give them advanced notice of tests. Regarding long-term projects or term papers, we could ask students to submit outlines and/or first chapters of the projects. We may also have to set aside class time for students to ask questions so as to get in the right mindset about doing a long-term assignment.

3 | **Greet Your Students at the Door and Welcome Them.** *"Not greeting your students everyday may be one of the biggest mistakes you could ever make."* —Annette Breaux

At the beginning of a class, teachers have a myriad of things that need to be done before the class begins. They need to put homework on the board, students from the previous period have questions, and teachers need some down time to breath. Yet it is really critically important that students feel welcome when they come into a classroom. Walmart hires individuals whose sole responsibility is to welcome you to the store. When you board an airplane, the flight attendant welcomes you to the store. Should we do anything less than to welcome our students to our classroom? Some of them have had to overcome major challenges in order to come to school. Some have had to deal with abuse, poverty, illness, or death in their family or with friends. We need to make them welcome. You might also make some personal comment in the welcome. "You look particularly pretty today. Did you comb your hair differently?" Or "I wanted to complement you on the way you behaved yesterday." Or "I noticed that you did particularly well on the quiz that I gave." I believe that you will notice a change in their attitude.

4 | **Involve Students in the Learning Process.** Students delight in being involved in the learning process. Moreover, people who are involved in their learning learn faster.

Have students write the end to stories in English classes. Give students a choice of books to read in English and social studies.

In history class, ask students, "What if the South had won the Civil War? What if Germany had won WWII? What if Al Gore had won the 2004 presidential election? "WHAT IF ... Hitler had won WWII or Jonas Salk had not found the poliovirus? What kinds of questions could you use for music, art, math, and English?

Bring an object into school and have the students identify it. In mathematics, it could be something as simple as a slide rule. You might bring an object into school and have the students make a story up about the object.

5 | **"I Taught My Dog How to Whistle."** David Langford tells the story "I taught my dog how to whistle. I did a really good job of teaching. But my dog cannot whistle."

In education we are measuring the wrong thing. We measure teaching and not learning. Supervisors observe teachers and say things like:

"Good lesson plan."
"Good pivotal questions."
"The students were all attentive."

"The classroom was well-decorated."
"Good final summary"

The real question to ask is: "Were the students learning?" We need to measure the performance of a teacher by measuring the success of the students they teach. When teaching a lesson, remember it is not only a question of how well you are teaching, but also a question of how well the students are learning.

In addition, we need to wean students from what I call "dependent learning" where the learning is based on the teacher's input rather than the student's output. Students need to move beyond passive or dependent education. In dependent learning, students are dependent on the instructor. The business world is increasingly becoming dependent on teamwork. But in classrooms across America we are still insisting on dependent, passive learning.

The following diagram depicts the three levels of student learning.

Inter-
dependent
Learning

Independent Learning

Passive or Dependent Learning

By using passive learning the responsibility for learning is formulated on the success of the teacher. The student has little or no responsibility. Go into the teachers lounge or faculty cafeteria of many middle and high schools and you will hear the teachers say: "Boy, did I work hard today. They didn't do their homework." Or, "they didn't study for their test." We have taken away the responsibility for learning from the students.

6 | **Independent Learning.** One of the ways of placing the responsibility of learning back on the students is by using "independent learning." The best example of this is when students are placed in front of computers and learn material on their own and at their own pace. This can be more satisfying to the student because computers do not place value judgments on the success of their work and they enjoy working with non-judgmental devices. At the same time though, the student may get off task and surf the Internet or play computer games. Some educators consider independent learning to be the highest form of student learning.

7 | **Interdependent Learning.** I believe the highest form of student learning is "interdependent learning," where students are dependent on each other for their learning success. Some examples would be working on a joint project or a joint class presentation. The business world is increasingly becoming dependent on teamwork.

While sharing of knowledge in the business world is called "teamwork," in the education world it is called "cheating." According to Dr. William Glasser, students learn the most when they teach others. I refer to this as interdependent learning. For me it is the highest form of learning, higher than independent learning. Independent learning is best exemplified by computer-based instruction. While there are major advantages in having students learn on computers, they miss the interaction of social activities. Interdependent learning has students helping or mentoring other students for the benefit of both. The slower learner reinforces their own learning, clarifies what they think they know, and aids a classmate. For the teacher, the benefit is that instead of working with 34 individual students, they are working with 17 teams. It is the ideal win-win situation. For the faster learner, this process not only reinforces their own learning but helps clarify things which they may not have clearly understood.

8 | **The Sounds of Learning.** I have had the privilege of visiting elementary, middle, and high schools in 49 states and eight countries. As I visit schools and classrooms in elementary schools, I hear the sound of learning. When I visit middle and high schools, too frequently, I hear the sound of teaching. In elementary schools, students help to direct their own learning processes. You see children who take delight in being in school. By the time they get to middle and high school, for many of them, the joy of learning has disappeared. Some sit with their heads on desks or even sleep. We have taken away the joy of learning from them. Secondary school teachers believe that we need to motivate them to learn. Elementary school teachers know that students are naturally motivated to learn. We have removed the desire to learn from them. We do not need to motivate students to learn. We need to find out what demotivates them to learn and remove those factors.

Children need to be the workers in education. In elementary schools they are! By the time they enter middle and high school, it is the teacher who is the worker. If you do not believe me, go into any middle or high school faculty lounge or staff cafeteria and listen to teachers who say, "*I* really worked hard today. They didn't study or do homework." We need to turn responsibility for learning back to students. The results of international examinations like the TIMMS (Third International Math and Science Survey) or PISA (Program for International Student Assessment) show that U.S. fourth grade students are ahead of most nations. By the eighth grade, we are in the middle of the pack. By the 12th grade we are near the bottom. Maybe it's because our students lack the motivation to learn because we've taken it away

9 | **Judging Students by the Content of Their Character.** In Dr. Martin Luther King Jr.'s famous "I Have A Dream" speech he said, "I have a dream that my four little children will one day live in a nation where they will not be judged by the color of their skin but by the content of their character." I recently saw a group of students dancing in wheelchairs and realized that there aren't any handicapped students. Only handicapping conditions which in most cases, can be overcome. By imposing our labels on children we frequently "see" these conditions before we see the students and start presuming what they can and cannot achieve. Each student is a cornucopia of various physical and behavioral traits. No single trait remotely defines any of us. This prejudice, or prejudgment clouds the achievement possibilities we expect from special education, minority, and poor students. We need to suspend judgment until we "see" what the individuals can achieve.

10 | **The Achievement Gap.** Achievement gaps exist among all kinds of students. They exist along racial, ethnic and socioeconomic lines as well as African American, Hispanic, and Native American children. While the gaps grew narrower between the 1970s and 1980s the research indicates that it has grown wider in recent years. Cultural factors play a role in the gaps including poverty, poor health care, mobility of the family, low educational levels of parents or guardians, lack of resources in the home (e.g., no place for students to study), parents who do not read to their children, and lack of books in the home. It is important to remember that many of these challenges are outside the control of classroom teachers, but others are in the domain of teachers.

Expect high quality work from *all* students. Remember, it is not the color of the balloon that determines how high it will go. It is what is inside that counts. It is imperative that teachers place the highest possible standards in front of children. Not all children will reach them but experienced teachers know that most children will strive to reach them if given the inspiration.

Provide extra help to those children who need it. The help needs to be provided to those students the minute a teacher identifies that a student has not mastered the material taught. Waiting until the end of the term or the end of the marking period makes little sense. Many subjects are "building block subjects." That is to say if a student doesn't understand or grasp a concept taught on Monday, she will be lost for the entire week, or term. If your school has a mentoring or tutoring program, use it. Remember that tutoring can be given before school begins, after the school day ends, on Saturdays or even during a lunch period.

Use data to identify student needs. Go over test material and homework to see where a student, a group of students, or the class failed to grasp a concept.

Do not track low income or ethnically diverse students into low-level classes. The U.S. Department of Education and the Southern Regional Education Board found that students perform at above their ability level when programmed into high-level classes. I know an elementary school teacher in Philadelphia who told her third grade low-level performing class that they were of such high caliber that they had been selected to learn Spanish. She placed signs around her classroom in Spanish identifying various objects. Guess what? The students learned to speak and write in Spanish.

11 | **Learn All Students' Names as Early as Possible.** We need to break down the bonds of anonymity that surrounds our students. We need to learn their names as early as possible. It shows respect.

An easy technique of remembering names that I have used is by using the name in class. If you see a student in the hall, stop them and say something to the effect, "I don't remember your name but aren't you in one of my classes. If they acknowledge, ask her what his or her name is. It will help you remember it.

Take pictures of your students and post them on a board and see if you (and your students) can identify who they are. Post their names below the picture so that other students can easily identify one another. (It also makes a terrific memento for you to remind you about who you have taught.)

12 **Transitional Students.** Data indicates that the highest dropout grade is the ninth. A study conducted in 450 high schools showed that 25% of ninth graders were not successful in moving on to the 10th grade. Another study conducted at Johns Hopkins University showed that a student who successfully completes ninth grade in a single year increase the likelihood of graduating by 85%. What can classroom teachers do to increase the success of ninth graders? A student's growing up has a tremendous impact on their education. Students leaving the cozy, cocooned environment of elementary school and moving on to the larger more impersonal middle or junior high school feel that no one cares about them. They need to be recognized for their talents and abilities. Teachers and counselors need to provide extra help in the development of academic and social skills. School administrators need to collaborate with feeder middle schools to clarify what the expectations for these incoming students. Articulation programs need to be held for both these students and their parents. The articulation program should include a tour of the building and the establishment of a one-to-one mentor program so that when the new student arrives at the school they are familiar with the layout of the building, where the lunchroom and bathrooms are, and they can identify at least one student who has been at the school. The mentors should be given a symbol (a jacket or an armband) so that the newly arrived student can immediately identify who is willing to provide assistance. Special tutoring services need to be provided possibly during lunch periods.

13 | **Look for Signs.** What does a bored student look like? Do you know how to recognize body language as well as students yawning? How many students in your class have their heads on their desk or may even be sleeping? We tend to blame that behavior on outside forces—like the fact that they were up late in the evening or they work after school—but the reality is that we may be a contributor to that behavior. For better or worse, we in education are contending with the competition of television, movies, video games, and the Internet. All of those activities require interactive participation while classroom performance is too frequently passive. Students need to be actively involved in their own learning. They are bored by passive learning activities. We need to look for signs of boredom. Identify the signs and act to avert them. Having students with their heads on desks may be as much our fault as theirs.

14 | **Taking a Risk.** Education is a relatively risk-free, stable job. And most educators are not risk takers. The *New York Times* recently asked its readers, "What was the greatest risk you have taken?" The answers were interesting and made me think that maybe we should be asking our at-risk students the same question. What do you think they might answer? How many of us can guess their responses? Maybe it is a question we should ask them once they get to know us better.

We can ask them to take a risk on what we are teaching and what we telling them about their future and how much their lives are dependent on success in the educational system.

15 | **Differentiated Instruction.** Get to know your students' learning styles. Be aware of the variety of learning styles. Some students are tactile or hands-on learners while others do well with the written word.

Some students study best alone; some in a group. When do they study best? In the morning? In the evening? Where do they do their best work? Where do they have difficulty?

Create the right classroom environment. Flexible seating charts. Don't put your weakest learners in back of the class. Develop a positive class culture with encouraging reinforcement of events that take place in the classroom.

Try mixing up groups. Occasionally group students by similar needs or interests. The next time change the group so that it is by mixed needs or interests. Allow students to leave a group if they are justified in feeling that they are out of place.

Test students on what they have or have not learned. Be aware that the prime focus of a test is to determine what to do next. If material has not been mastered, then there may be a need to reteach it before moving forward with the curriculum.

Differentiate your questions by developing higher-level thinking questions for students who can answer them and then adjust some questions for students with greater needs. Adjust the response time for students who need more time to process the question.

16 **Classroom Testing.** Traditional testing goes that if too many students fail a test, we curve the grades. If too many students pass the test, how many of us believe that we were just terrific at teaching and taught the students well? There are certain things we can do to improve test grades:

1. First we need to provide guidance to students to show them how to do better.

2. We need to emphasize that we need to teach students **how to think as well as what to think**. There may be more than one right answer. Teachers need to ask more "why" questions and fewer "when" or "what" questions. "Why" questions probe for a deeper understanding of information. "When" or "what" questions simply rely on a regurgitation of information which is easily found in libraries and computers.

3. We should establish a test sharing policy with other teachers teaching the same subject or the same grade.

4. Students should have a role in evaluating their own progress, establish learning goals and techniques for reaching those goals.

5. There are a variety of assessment techniques. Written tests are not the only one. We can use classroom discussions, oral reports, role-playing, as well as, formal tests.

6. Teachers need to provide specific feedback as to how individual students can improve their grades.

17 | **Differentiate the Homework.** Some students need more complex homework than others. Have the brighter students do in-depth research on a fewer number of questions. Try to avoid boredom which research has shown is the prime enemy of classroom instruction.

18 | **When Graduates Return, Have Them Teach a Class.** Let them explain to students what they are doing now that they have left school. What skills are they using that the school taught them? What skills are they lacking that would have better prepared them for college, the workplace, or the military. Not only will this give the graduate an ego boost, but it also shows off the success that graduates have after graduating from your school. As a reward, take them to the teacher's cafeteria and treat them to lunch. Let them meet their former teachers and have the teachers ask the graduate what could they have done better to prepare the students for the world after school.

19 | **Jimmy, Stay After Class and See Me.** Making that statement is frequently for something punitive. At the end of each class period, ask one student to stay for a moment and complement him on something. Or tell the student you missed them if she were absent. This will demonstrate that you have a concern for students. And they will spread the word.

20 | **Lend Students Pens, Pencils, and Paper.** None of us are perfect. Students will forget the equipment they need in order to work. We can become emotional and decide to punish them by saying something like, "Because you didn't bring a pen you just sit there and watch the other students work." Who is being punished? Ultimately it is us because these students will be taking examinations. I used to lend students a pen or paper. I took a shoe as a deposit which insured that I would get the pen back.

I used to attend workshops at hotels or convention centers. At the end of the presentation, I used to take all unclaimed pads or pens. Or I would tell the vendors at the end of a conference, that I would be willing to lighten their load home by taking the pens or pads they were distributing and give them as prizes for academic achievement to my students.

21 | **"Stupid" Questions.** Encourage students to ask questions when they do not understand something that has been taught, tested, or given as homework. Give students a respectful answer to their questions. Do not put down students who ask "stupid" questions. The only stupid question is the one not asked.

22 | **Technology.** Technology is only one tool in the teacher's toolbox. It should not be used as if it were the only one. The goal of using technology, as any other tool, is to improve student achievement and learning. Too often technology is employed as an electronic book with various "bells and whistles." Many teachers lack the knowledge of which software to use in classrooms. Ask colleagues, friends, and school and public librarians for advise about the best computer software. Find the tech "guru" in the school and ask him/her for advice about using computers. Use the resource section that appears at the end of this book for URLs (Uniform Resource Locators) that teachers can use. Have students use the Internet to connect to other students around the country and around the world to gather information about different cultures and different techniques of learning.

Computers are not the only technology for educators to use. Many classroom teachers use PowerPoint or Keynote software to deliver lessons. With fonts, you need to be consistent and use large type! The easiest font to read is either Arial Black (for facts and information) or Times New Roman (for quotes and stories). The rule of thumb for slides is that 30-point should be the smallest. Graphics can be obtained, free of charge from Google. Go to the top menu and choose "images." Type in the name of the person or object you seek in the search box. At last look, Microsoft Office Online (http://office.microsoft.com/enus/clipart/default.aspx) had 150,000 pieces of clipart. You can make slides stand out by using 66-point font.

If you are showing videos in class you need not show the whole video. Show a snippet of the film and direct student learning to what they have seen. There are enough video stores and sources like Netflix for students who are interested in seeing the entire film. It is easy enough to point out the theme or character development without having to show 2 weeks of "War and Peace."

We know that students watch television and go to the movies. Why not direct their learning and have them write a short essay on what they have seen. We can ask them why person Y was chosen as the leader of the group or why person X was "kicked off the island."

23 | Keep Your Eyes on the Stars, but Your Feet Firmly Planted on Earth.

When I was a counselor, a young lady came to see me. I asked her what she planned to do after graduation. She said that she wanted to be a psychiatrist. I said that the first requirement in being a psychiatrist was knowing how to spell it. Without a blink, she asked if she could be a nurse instead. I said, "You could be anything that you want to be. But you do not like math or science, two requirements for becoming a nurse. And you do not like school. Do you have any idea how long it takes to become a nurse?"

Many young people do not have any idea what they would like to be after they graduate nor do they have any idea of the requirements to obtain their dreams and goals. While we should not shoot down their dreams, it is our responsibility as educators to educate them as to the demands of the job and the training it will take.

A young man on our football team came to see me about life after graduation. I asked what were his plans and he said that he was a "superb football player" and would be chosen to play in the National Football League (NFL) upon graduation from college. He expected to obtain a full football scholarship to college because he was such a good player. I said to him, "Let's play a scenario. You get accepted to college on a full football scholarship. Is that possible?" "Absolutely," was his response. "You go out for your first football practice and you rip your Achilles tendon and cannot play football again. Is that possible?" "Yes", he replied. I then asked, "What is your fall back position? What do you do next?"

Our young people do not make contingency plans. They do not think beyond the next visible hurdle. They do not think that they are vulnerable and susceptible to disease, accidents, and whatever life may bring. Frequently, they think they can cram their way through life as they do for examinations. Our at-risk learners are the most vulnerable. They most often lack role models to guide them in making decisions. It is our responsibility to connect the world of school to the world of work.

24 | **Call Students if They Are Absent for An Extended Period of Time.** There are several reasons to do this. First, and most important, you are showing your concern. In addition, you might find out that there was a death in the family or serious illness. By giving absent students the homework they missed you prevent them from falling behind. You might ask another student for permission to photocopy their class notes. This will insure that students take notes in class in order to help their classmates succeed.

25 | **English Language Learners (ELL).** Educators are dealing with an increasing number of English language learners. The U.S. Department of Education estimates that the number of ELL students has doubled from 2.2 million to 4.4 million during the 1990s. Several practical pieces of advice: First, do not lose your patience in dealing with these children. Remember that they are going through two learning processes at the same time. First they are learning the language and then they are learning the subject you are teaching. It will take some of them longer to learn than others. Some of these children are also learning the Western or English alphabet. Some Chinese, Arab, Russian, or Turkish students use a different alphabet than we do. Avoid overly correcting their spoken grammar. See if you can find another student who can serve as a mentor to help them. Use simple sentences and language in dealing with them. Compliment them when they succeed but compliment them even more when they try. Imagine if the situation was reversed and you were in their country trying to learn their language and subjects.

26 | **Weekly Report Cards.** One of teachers' biggest complaints is that they never have enough time. Jeffrey J. Mayer wrote a book in 1991, titled, *If You Haven't Got the Time to Do It Right, When Will You Find the Time to Do It Over*? We need to take the time to give out weekly report cards, especially for those at risk of failing. Waiting for end-of-term or end-of-year examinations simply indicate that failure of the student is imminent. Report cards issued after a marking period ends generally indicate failure. By taking the time to give students a written or oral weekly or biweekly report card and telling them what they can do to improve, you short circuit the failing nature of the traditional report card cycle.

Students and their parents need to know as soon as we know, that they are not doing well. Develop a form (possibly with some other colleagues) requiring a parent signature, to be distributed to students who need to improve their attendance, punctuality, discipline, homework, or their test scores. Do not send it to those students who are doing well. Keep track of those that were sent home. Make a copy of them so in case they were not returned you will have a record. You might want to send the note home by e-mail. This will limit the amount of additional work you will need to do. Additionally, you might want to send home notes to parents of those students whose work is improving, as well.

27 | **Reviewing for Tests.** Reviewing for tests is frequently boring for both students and the teacher. I used to prepare a review list of words and phrases that I gave to the students the day before the review. I told the students that each of the words on the sheet would be on the test and that they had to study each of the words for the review. The next day I divided the class into two groups. We would then play "Jeopardy." I would call a student from one team and give him a word from the review list. If the individual would give an answer that satisfied the judge (me) the team would get a point. If a member of the opposing team would add anything of value then the second team would get a point. Points would not be deduced for wrong answers or a lack of an answer. However, I would point out to the student who did not respond, "It is obvious that you need to study that word because it will be on tomorrow's test." I did this in a high school, so the bell ended the game. The winning team received "extra credit." Students were excited and the "nerds" were valued for their presence on the team.

There are a number of variations that can be used:

- A variation of this would pit the males against the females.
- Depending on class size, two teams can be selected and "Family Feud" can be used as the teaching technique.
- There are a variety of Web sites which allow teacher's to create crossword puzzles that students may use to study for tests. (See the Resource Section at the end of the book.)

28 | What Do the Following Three-Letter Combinations Have in Common? BLL, LST, MSS, PCK? (The answer is at the end of this page.) Teachers find that they are in competition with television and if they wish to succeed, especially with nontraditional students, they need to involve them in their learning. There are several mind games that I used. As classroom educators know, some lessons run long (go beyond the class period) and others fall short. I used to tell my students that if the lesson ran short and I was happy that the lesson had been covered, I would give them a mind game to play in class. A list of mind game books is in the Resources Section of this book.

The puzzles come in a variety of subject areas: mathematics, science, social studies, and English. The puzzles not only break up the daily routine for students, as well as for teachers, but they also encourage students to study and do their homework so there will be classroom time for mind games.

The answer to the three letter combinations above: Add any vowel to the three letters (with the exception of "y") to make a variety of words.

29 | **Personalize and Align Education.** Here are several suggestions on how you can personalize and align education:

- In social studies, ask students to find out the requirements for jobs 20, 50, and 100 years ago and ask why.
- In math, ask students to find out the cost of things 20, 50, and 100 years ago and ask them to determine percentage increases. Compare it to income levels of the time.
- In English, ask students to create a newspaper that teenagers would read.
- Send birthday cards to students. Use the role book or school database to identify birthdays. Many of today's children have parents or relatives who do not acknowledge the children's birthdays. Many of today's children are in merged families, foster homes, have been kicked out of their own homes, or are homeless. Acknowledging who they are shows that you care about them as individuals. There are software programs that allow you to print birthday cards. If you are working in a high school or middle school, you might want to simply post the month's birthdays on a flip chart. While students might say that this is childish, deep down they appreciate it.
- Don't judge students by outward appearances. Today's children dress differently, have body piercings, and tattoos. Some teachers judge students by their appearance rather than what is inside their heads. Don't place a value judgment on outside physical impressions. Remember what

your mother thought about how you and your friends dressed.

30 | **How Many of You Like to Eat Steak or Fish?**
Imagine you are a student in a classroom on a typical day (typical because everyday is the same). You walk into class, you sit at your desk, and the teacher tells you to open your textbook. The teacher lectures and you take notes. You read a chapter. You do lots of worksheets. You memorize the notes you need to study for Friday's test. You are expected to be interested, keep quiet, and master the material. Imagine doing that every single day for 180 days.

We need to vary our lessons, teaching techniques, and we need to get students actively involved in their own learning.

31 | **Vary Your Teaching Strategies.** "The mediocre teacher tells. The good teacher explains. The superior teacher demonstrates. The great teacher inspires." —William Arthur Ward

What kind of teacher are you?

32 | "We Don't Want to Brag" Bulletin Board.

Everyone wants to see positive things happening. Establish a "brag" bulletin board for each of your classes. If something good happens to one of the students or their family, post this information on the bulletin board (i.e., their family had another child, a brother or sister graduated from college, or their brother is proudly serving in the military.) For many of these youngsters there is so little to celebrate in their lives that every opportunity to celebrate is an opportunity to positively reinforce success.

Use bulletin boards in your classroom, your office, and in the halls. Decorate them with student work or graphs showing improvement. Graph lines should always be going up. Don't show a decrease in dropout rates but an improvement in the graduation rate.

School administrators can have a brag bulletin board for the school showing positive achievements of students, graduates, and all staff members. Too many schools that I have visited only demonstrate the success of their athletes. While this is an important achievement, it represents only a small proportion of the school.

33 **Schools Need to Be Inviting Places to Visit.** Schools, especially large ones, are intimidating to people who visit, whether they are parents, the community at large, or simply people who wish to visit. We put up an electronic bulletin board which reads, "Through these doors walk the finest people in the world: Our students, their parents, our staff, and our guests." That was the first thing you saw as you entered our building. It provided a positive message to those who entered. Teachers can put a similar greeting over the door of their classroom.

34 **Take Help Wherever You Can Get It.** How many of you have ever observed other teachers? The best ideas I've ever gotten I've "stolen" from other teachers. The best help I ever received was from my colleagues down the hall.

35 **Make Your Objectives Clear.** Imagine going on vacation without knowing where you are going. Imagine a doctor performing surgery without an objective. Do your students know what they are expected to learn from the lesson you are teaching? Do *you* know what you're expecting students to learn from the lesson? Lessons must have a clear, measurable objective.

36 **Lecturing.** Lecturing is the least effective method of instruction, yet it is the most often used. You do not learn how to swim by being lectured by an expert on swimming. Don't only use the textbook to teach from. Consider what you remember from school. Was it the textbooks that you had or was it the "stories" the teachers talked about? The ineffective teacher uses the textbook to tell her what to teach, how to teach it, when to teach it, and what questions to ask. No textbook has an exact correlation to the district's curriculum. That does not mean you should not use the textbook. It means that the textbook is a tool. Be creative. Vary your teaching techniques.

37 **Relevance.** Relate what you are teaching to "real-life" connections. Many of us teach something because it's in the syllabus or in the curriculum but fail to comprehend why we are teaching it. If we do not understand why we are teaching some material, then students have a valid question when they ask, "why are we learning this?" We need to connect what we teach to the relevance of why we teach it. We cannot respond to the question by saying, "You are learning it because it may be on the test." Or by saying, "you may need this later on in your life."

38 | **Homework Overload.** There is such a thing as homework overload. How much time should students spend doing homework? There have been a number of studies about the effectiveness of homework. Many believe that homework helps to deepen student learning and develop thinking skills. It also teaches responsibility, managing time, and study habits. Others believe that homework takes away time from childhood play, overburdens students, and takes away from family time. Some parents feel it is given to students to bury them in work.

The research on the effectiveness of giving homework and its impact on student achievement is in disagreement and sometimes contradictory. Some of the highest performing nations in the world like Finland and Japan assign less homework than we do in America.

Make homework interesting, purposeful, and doable. On one of your slow days, try doing the homework that you have assigned to students. See how long it takes you to do it. Add anywhere from 15 minutes to a half an hour for your students to do it. Did it take too long to do? Was it relevant to what the students had learned or would learn the next day? Was it interesting? Or was it simply, "Read pages 1-14 and answer questions 1, 3, 4, 5, 6, and 7 on page 17?"

You need to know why you are assigning homework. Is it achieving the objectives that you had in mind? Research shows that the most effective homework either prepares students for future lessons or reinforces and clarifies lessons that have just been taught. Some students will tell you that they understand all of the work at the end of the lesson but when they go home they find that they did not understand key concepts.

Do not collect homework unless you plan to do something with it. For teachers in middle and high school this is difficult to do with 130–150 students. I found that it was possible to check one or two of the most important homework questions so I understood whether students got the key points of a lesson or whether I needed to reteach material. If the homework covered new material and I found that many students had omitted the question, the first thing I did on the next day was to go over the question. This allowed students to fill in the answer and made it possible for the lesson to go smoothly.

What does the research say about the amount of homework to be done? On average, Americans students have 1 hour of homework a night. But averages cover up a great deal of variation. Research indicates that older students benefit from more homework than younger students. But too much homework diminishes its effectiveness. For students in high school, 1½ to 2½ hours seems the optimum. For middle school students, less than 1 to 1½ hours per night (not per subject.) Research findings also conclude that it is not the amount of homework given but the amount of homework *completed* that raises student achievement.

Maintain open lines of communication with parents about how long it takes their child to do homework. If the child takes too long to do homework, it may indicate that the child is having other problems in school that the teacher may be unaware of. You might want to develop a form asking parents if their child

- completed the homework easily and independently;

- had difficulty understanding what was asked in the homework;
- had difficulty completing the homework; or
- had difficulty focusing on the assignment.

I suggest that schools need to provide assistance to students who need help doing homework. Some schools/districts have established homework assistance helplines. One such example would be the Miami-Dade Dial-A-Teacher on Line (http://www.dial-a-teacher.com/index .html) that can be used as a benchmark.

Maybe you can get together with colleagues on the same grade level and agree that not everyone assigns a great deal of work on the same day. For example, on Monday, social studies teachers will assign homework; on Tuesday, math; on Wednesdays, science and English, and so on.

When children come home from school, the first thing many parents ask, "Do you have homework?" We need to insure the pattern of homework given. Parents need to know if homework is given everyday. Are special projects assigned during the school term and how long they will take to be completed? Will homework be graded? Will there be a need for parent signatures on the homework?

39 | **Should All Children Go to College?** All children should be prepared with the skills they need to succeed with in life. We can no longer afford to track students. If students show that they are capable of working with their hands as well as their heads then we need to give them the skills that will enable them to succeed at that. For example, if a student wishes to become an automobile repairman, they need to know math, as well as how to run computers. There are at least 12 computers in every car presently on the market. They need to know how to read car repair manuals. As a classroom educator, you have a responsibility of raising students to their highest level of success.

40 | **There Is a Difference Between Boys and Girls.** What do little boys like to read? What do little girls like to read? We know that boys like to read different things than do girls. Boys like sports and cars and girls like to read about movie stars and makeup. This is not a sexist statement. Be aware of gender differences in assigning books.

Another difference was pointed out by a colleague who, when looking at a boy's notebook, described it as a "black hole." Boys need assistance (not to exclude some girls) to get things organized. I suggest that you train students to organize their notebooks into five sections.

- ♦ Notes
- ♦ Homework
- ♦ Handouts

- Tests and Quizzes
- Blank paper

41 | **What Are Their Strengths?** Identify three to five strengths of your at-risk learners. In my workshop, attendees came up with the following answers:

- They are survivors;
- Can flourish with encouragement;
- Creative;
- Intelligent;
- Holistic learners;
- Accepting of differences; and
- Leaders.

What positive strengths could you add to the list? We need to take advantage of these strengths. But first, we need to identify them. One of the smartest mathematics students I knew was a student who was alleged to be committing illegal acts. Not only was he good in math but he also possessed superb leadership skills. We involved him in the school math-tutoring program to provide assistance to struggling students. This turned his life around and those of his fellow students. He gave up the illegal activities, went on to complete school, college, and is now a productive member of society.

42 | Identify 3 to 5 Challenges of Your At-Risk Learners.

Attendees at my workshops have identified:

- Low motivation;
- Trauma-ridden;
- Defiant;
- Blamers;
- Victim;
- Thrill seekers;
- Risk takers;
- Impulsive;
- Loyalty;
- Negative self-image;
- Manipulative; and
- Poor choice making.

If we had these challenges in our lives, could we overcome them? When we teach at-risk students many of us are unaware of the challenges they had to overcome merely to come to school. I am not saying we need to teach down to them, but merely to provide an understanding of the obstacles in their lives.

43 | **Knowing What to Teach.** Knowing what not to teach is probably as important as knowing what to teach. Coaches go into a game with a game plan; doctor's do the same; lawyers not only prepare the questions but the answers as well. Remember, you cannot teach everything. Do not try to. America's textbooks have grown in size exponentially as information has expanded. In your lesson plan, prepare the information that you wish to teach. Also prepare information for students who wish to learn more.

44 | **Make Extensive Use of Bulletin Boards.** Using graphs, post class improvements on test scores, attendance, homework, and so on. Have graphs going up, not down. There is a negative psychological effect to seeing line graphs going down. Don't show a decrease in absences. Show an increase in attendance. Consider use of "scatter diagrams." After giving a test, design a graph showing student test scores (on the vertical axis) compared to attendance (on the horizontal axis). There will probably be a correlation to students who attend regularly with students who score well on tests. You might also want to compare test scores (on the vertical axis) compared to homework completion (on the horizontal axis). There will probably be a correlation to students who do homework regularly with students who score well on tests. While this may be common sense to us, for students who are visual learners it will make clear what we have been saying to them for a long time.

45 | **Take a Temperature Check.** Have students use a "thumbs up/thumbs down" method on whether they understand the material you are teaching. If the majority indicates that they do not understand the subject matter, find out why and reteach. This is especially critical in "building block" subjects like math, science, and foreign language, where if you lose students on Monday they will not understand Tuesday's lesson.

46 | **Free Things.** Get free material for classroom bulletin boards from the Armed Forces, NASA, movie theaters, and private industry.

47 | **Unprepared Students.** Students occasionally do not come prepared to class. Some students do not bring pens, pencils or paper to class. Some teachers say, "Since you did not come prepared, sit there." This may lead to the bored student disrupting the class. Also, who is being punished, you or the student? A student who is not taking notes cannot do homework and will fall behind the class. If a student needs to borrow a pen or pencil or paper, have them leave something personal with you. I used a shoe.

48 | **Returning Tests.** Always be the person who returns test papers. Leave them on the desk face down. This causes fewer problems in the long run as well as not embarrassing students who do not do well.

49 | **Getting Student Information.** Use colored index cards to get student information. On one side of the card write the last name in large letters, followed by the first name. On the other side of the card list address, phone number, contact names of guardians, e-mail, and parents' cell phone numbers.

50 | **Increasing Attendance.** Hold special activities on Fridays and Mondays to encourage attendance. Find out what excites students and use those events to encourage student attendance. Find out the causes of student tardies and attendance problems. Use the data to change student behavior. For example, if students do not attend on the Monday after a big football game, do not schedule the teaching of new material which if students miss, they will be lost for the rest of the week or term.

51 | **Student-Led Parent Conferences.** Most schools discourage students from attending parent-teacher conferences. I believe that this is a mistake. Students should be encouraged to come with their parent/guardian. In addition, they should be trained in how to lead these conferences. Teachers can also prepare a "crib sheet" with questions that students need to raise at these conferences. By having a student conduct the conference, the conference becomes less confrontational and puts the student in the position of explaining excessive lateness, absences, and low grades on tests.

52 | **Curriculum Alignment.** I have never understood why teachers in social studies were teaching American history, while teachers of English were teaching English or French literature. Get together with a few colleagues to see if it is possible to align your curricula with theirs. For example, teachers of social studies, art, English, music, and possibly science can all "be on the same page" when teaching material. It will make it easier for students to understand that when Columbus sailed for the New World, he didn't fly across the Atlantic because airplanes had not yet been invented. What music did he listen to in Spain before he left or after he returned? What impact did the Inquisition (as shown in the art of the time) have on his departure or in gaining a crew to come with him? Not only will this clarify information in the students' minds but it will make the jobs of the teachers involved easier as well.

53

Student Diversity. Increasingly schools have to deal with students who come from diverse religious, cultural, and economic backgrounds, and with wide ranges of abilities and skills. Students process information and act differently based on previous interests, learnings, and backgrounds. It therefore becomes essential that classroom educators know where they are going and how to get there by aligning what they are teaching with federal, state, and local curriculum and syllabi. There also needs to be a realization that a single approach toward instruction is not as effective as multiple approaches to content and a variety of classroom-instruction techniques including whole-class, group, and individual instruction.

Instruction needs to focus on student understanding and not on assessment. Students need to have the ability to demonstrate both an understanding of concepts as well as methods of implementation. It is equally as important that students get the right answer as well as having the ability to detail the method of obtaining the right answer.

We need to discover what matters to students so that we can have them link what they have learned with something that's important to them.

54 | **The Need for Student Planning.** Ask your students, "How many of you have ever gone into a store and the thing that you wanted to buy was not in stock? Didn't you feel they should have planned to have ordered more so they would have it when you come in? What would happen if the farmer hadn't planted enough and the price of corn had gone up?" While cramming for a test is better than not studying at all, things can go wrong. An emergency might arise or a friend suddenly gets tickets for a concert that you've wanted to see. Students need to make plans for schoolwork just as they make plans for the weekend.

55 | **Listen First, Then Give Advice—The Story of Hector.**[1] Hector arrived at our school at the beginning of his 10th grade year. That, in itself was a bit unusual because we are a traditional 9-12 high school. The dean, in an intake interview asked him why his principal had sent him to our school.

Hector said that in his ninth grade he had given up attending his previous high school, had attended for only 21 days, had been arrested five times for dealing narcotics, and had been "kicked out" of his former school.

The dean looked at his record and said, "For 9 years, you were an excellent student. What happened last year?" Hector replied, "My father was dying and I wanted to pay for the funeral so I dealt drugs to pay for it." The dean said "Well, now that you are here we want

---

1.   Not his real name.

you to graduate." Hector said, "I don't need school. I can make more money on the street." The dean said that might be true but "What is your life expectancy on the street?" Hector replied, "Three years." The dean said, "If you want to live beyond 3 years, go see Schargel."

Hector came to see me and we got him into our "Quality Student" program. He graduated on time but was not the valedictorian or salutatorian. He graduated with an 81% grade point average. We were able to get him an interview with a near-by college and a job with a business that we had a partnership agreement with. He was accepted to the college on full scholarship and the business agreed to hire him for summer work to pay for his school expenses as long as he maintained a B average. He came to see me and thank us for getting him into the school and for getting him a summer job. He said, "Schargel, thank you but I cannot accept the school scholarship or the job. Too many people know me in Brooklyn and I know too many of them. Either they will kill me or I'll kill one of them. You have to get me out of town."

I knew a college dean and called him. I said, "You need to interview Hector. Not because he's a minority. He is. Not because he's poor. He is. But because he's Hector."

The school held a cake sale to get Hector to the upstate New York college and some "dress-up" clothing. Hector was accepted to the college.

I got a phone call on October 30, Halloween night, the first year Hector was in the school. The college dean said to me, "You have to do something about Hector." There were two thoughts that ran through my mind. First, Hector had been arrested for dealing drugs or stealing school property. Second, I saw myself driving upstate for 3 hours on Halloween night and 3 hours back because I knew that Hector's mother didn't own a car. I asked the dean what Hector had done. The dean replied, "He's been elected as the freshman representative to the student government. He's the most popular freshman on campus. Do you have any more Hectors at the school?" I asked to speak to Hector and said, "Hector, when you come back to the city to visit your mom, I need to know how we can clone you. How do we produce more Hectors? What did we do right?"

Hector said, "I will answer those questions only if you take me to an expensive restaurant."

When Hector came to lunch at the restaurant—an expensive one. He said, "The dean was the first person who ever *asked* me what I needed instead of *telling* me what I needed to do."

The story doesn't end there. Hector graduated and went to Hollywood, California where he is employed at a top Hollywood studio. He makes more in 1 year than I made in several years of teaching. I had a speaking engagement in Hollywood and called him. I said that I was coming to Hollywood and would like to have lunch with him. I wanted to go to an expensive restaurant and I expected him to pay. He did.

We need to listen first, before we give advice.

Professional Growth

I prefer to call this section Professional Growth as opposed to Professional Development. For me, professional development is an organized, top-down driven process. It meets the needs of those outside the instructional body but too frequently fails to meet the needs of the school or the district. It has a short-term focus while teachers have their attention on other matters. I see professional growth as percolating from the teacher and is classroom driven by those who deliver the instruction.

56 | **Making Rules.** Keep the number of rules short. The list should be clear, unambiguous, and consistently enforced. It will not take your students long to test you and them. Establish a graduated series of steps for infractions of rules. Involve students in establishing rules. Sending a child to the dean or the principal to be disciplined only diminishes your power in the eyes of the students. Children want and need structure. If a student breaks a rule, there must be a consequence. Discipline is not about problem solving, but rather about problem prevention. Do not abuse your power by making rules that you cannot enforce. "If you talk again to me that way, I will have you expelled."

57 | **On-the-Job Training.** Imagine someone teaching you how to swim by giving you instructions while on land. You read books on the subject. You study charts. You take a written test on how to swim and do very well. Would you know how to swim? You can take all of the courses you need in college on how to teach. You can read all of the books on teaching. You can see all of the videos and see people teaching. But you need to experience it for yourself. What helps people to teach? The data indicate that five things are the key:

1. **Mentoring with an experienced colleague(s):** Find someone whom you trust and whom you believe has greater teaching abilities than you. Ask him/her if they will help you to improve your skills.

2. **Observe other teachers:** Ask some of your fellow teachers if you could sit in on their classes so that you could learn proven instructional techniques.
3. **Team up of with teachers in a similar position:** If you are a noncertified teacher trying to become certified, find other noncertified teachers to form a study and observation group.
4. **Supportive administrators:** Most, if not all administrators want to help you perfect your skills. If things go easier for you, things will go easier for them. Ask for their help.
5. **Keep up with the latest research:** Take additional in-serve or college courses. Join professional organizations like the National Dropout Prevention Center, the Southern Regional Education Board, Phi Delta Kappa, and the American Society for Curriculum Development. Read their journals and attend their conferences.

58 **Highly Effective Teaching.** The new emphasis of state testing and No Child Left Behind has placed an emphasis on "Highly Qualified Teachers." A highly qualified teacher is one who knows their material. Yet we have all had highly qualified teachers who were incapable of teaching students. What we need in addition to highly qualified teachers are highly effective teachers. Rand researchers have identified characteristics of highly effective teachers:

1. Take personal responsibility for student learnings and look for ways they can be more effective.
2. Have high standards and expectations for all students. How do you communicate your standards to students? Set high standards and help students reach them. Let them help you determine what an "A" or a "90" is.
3. Provide a variety of feedback mechanisms to help students analyze their work and come to their own conclusions.
4. See low-achieving students as capable of learning and developing nonadversarial relationships with adults.
5. Set learning goals for both themselves and their students.

59 | **Starting Out on the Right Foot.** Teachers love teaching so much that they jump into teaching content immediately after giving school and classroom rules. Take some time before jumping in to explain to children why you love teaching. Tell them what your expectations of them are and what they can expect from you and your class. Tell your students what you expect, show them how you expect things to be done. Don't leave it up to them and do not make it a mystery. Share with them your enthusiasm for teaching and your excitement about having them in your class. Express your belief that all of them will be successful.

60 | **Loving What You Love to Do.** If you are a middle or high school teacher, explain why you love the subject that you teach. Then find out what they love. You might want to give to them an index card and get their contact information. Get their e-mail address and the e-mail address of their parent or guardian. Ask the students to write down what they love to do or what they hope to do when they graduate. Use the information when teaching a lesson. For example, if you find out that a young lady wants to become a nurse or a doctor and you teach science, ask if she knows what sciences she will have to take in order to become a nurse. If a male student wishes to become a pilot, ask if he knows the job requirements.

61 | **Getting Acquainted.** At one of the first class meetings, pair up students and have them get acquainted with one another. Have them switch partners after 5 minutes. Spend the rest of the period having one student introduce someone they met and discuss what interesting things they found out about the person (i.e., hobbies, number of children in the family, student's career aspirations, what they would do if they suddenly received $1,000,000). Have the students establish a "buddy" list in case one of them is absent, or misses an assignment.

62 | **Time Management.** When I ask teachers what is the greatest problem that they face, the greatest response I get is that, "I don't have the time to do it all." How do you build instructional time into your schedule? First, plan your day, period, week, and school year. Guard and protect instructional time. Guard and protect your personal time. It is possible that teachers can work a 24-hour day and still not be able to finish all the things they need to do. The worst thing that can happen is burnout due to overwork. Try to stop unnecessary class interruptions that distract you from teaching. Student learning and classroom instruction are paramount and are the reasons why schools were started. Teach things once and review only if students fail to master material.

63 | Creating Effective Teachers.

High stakes state testing and the demands of No Child Left Behind demand "highly qualified teachers," yet how many of us have had teachers who were highly qualified (They knew their subject material) but couldn't teach? What constitutes an effective teacher? We have all had teachers who we can say have made a major difference in our lives. Stop reading for a moment and think of that teacher and then ask yourself what quality or qualities that teacher had that made such an impact. Do you have a list? Here are some of the responses I have had in my workshops:

+ "He treated me as an individual."
+ "She saw the potential that I had and expected me to reach that potential."
+ "He had a good sense of humor."
+ "He provided feedback which allowed me to see the correct things I was doing and the things I needed to improve."
+ "She was strict and made us see the advantage in having us learn."

The question then becomes one of frequently reminded ourselves of these attributes and modeling them.

64 **Take a Lawyer's Advice.** Never ask a question that you don't know the answer to. Remember this in preparing a lesson plan. This technique will help you develop questions. Ask more "why" questions than "when," "what," or "how" questions. "Why" questions probe deeper thought and require more than one-word answers. It is important to gain factual information as well, but it is equally important for students to gain knowledge and wisdom. Many of the questions you ask have more than one right answer. The exchange in a classroom usually is teacher-student, teacher-student, and teacher to student. I believe it should be teacher to student to student to student, to student.

65 **Be Prepared.** This is not only the Boy Scout's motto; it should be every teacher's as well. Imagine if you went into the hospital for surgery and when the doctor came to see you he was unprepared. Imagine how upset you would be. Teachers are as professional as doctors and need to come to class organized and well prepared. Plan every minute of your day before hand.

66 | **Be Flexible But Not Double Jointed.** Being flexible will help you to deal with the unexpected. Experienced teachers know what is commonly referred to as Murphy's Law: "If something can go wrong, it will." The best laid plans will go awry. Things happen: students will come late to class or there could be interruptions from the public address system.

67 | **Start Out on the Right Foot.** Have some type of clearly marked seating chart to avoid confusion as to where students should sit. Make it clear to students that the seating plan will be changed based on your perception of what is the best learning environment. Ask which students need to sit up front in order to better see the board. Do not allow potential troublemakers to sit in back of the class. Look at a student's body language. It speaks as loudly as a scream.

68 | **Set High Expectations.** Set high expectations for **ALL** children. No child ever rose to low expectations. Not every child can reach your expectation, but if you have set the stage for the right environment, students will reach beyond *their* expectation of what they can achieve.

69 | **A Spoon Full of Sugar.** Students admire someone who is pleasant, kind, and considerate. Say to students, "please sit down," instead of "take your seats!" When you pass out books, hand them to students instead of dropping them on the desk. Greet your students at the door and welcome them. Walmart has the right idea. Anytime you go to Walmart the first person you see when you enter the store is a greeter who will say, "Welcome to Walmart." When you board an airplane, the flight attendant will say, "Welcome aboard." At the end of the flight the pilot will say, "Thank you for flying so and so airline." Can we do any less? Many of our students have had to overcome many hurdles to get to school. We may never know what obstacles they've overcome. Why not be pleasant and welcome them to your class?

70 | **Your Office.** "Rules are devised to set limits, to help maintain order, and to protect people." —Annette Breaux.

Confront bad behavior. Don't ignore it. Handle discipline problems in your "office." (Teachers do not believe they have an office, but they do. It is just outside the front door.) Do not embarrass students in front of their peers. You may win the battle but you will definitely lose the war. Avoid power struggles with students. You will lose even if you win. Attack the problem not the person. Never say "what's wrong with you!" One out of every 10 students is abused. That means in a class of 30 you could have three students dealing with abuse; out of 150 students you could have 15. Say instead, "I noticed that you are struggling with your work, is there anything I can do to help?"

71 | **Consistent Consequences.** Have students help establish guidelines of behavior. Doing so helps them to assume ownership of the guidelines. Hold students accountable for their behavior with *consistent* consequences. Ask yourself if the punishment fits the crime? The punishment must equal the infraction—not more, not less. Remember, rules provide structure and for many youngsters, especially the at-risk, there isn't much structure in their lives. Do not overly punish and do not punish the class for the actions of one individual or a group of individuals.

72 | **What Is the Purpose of a Mission Statement?** How many of you have classroom mission statements? What should you put into a classroom mission statement? Why not take some time and develop one? I would like to suggest that you use the following statement as a template: "As a result of taking this class ..." Students will be able to finish the sentence. As a result, they will assume ownership to a mission they helped develop.

73 | **Make Learning Fun.** Work is a four-letter word. Fun is a three-letter word. We know that people learn more when they are having fun. Teaching is also easier when it is fun for you as well. When I started teaching I was told, "Don't smile until Xmas". As silly as that sounds, many educators practiced it. Some of them may still be at your school.

Learn to laugh and have the students laugh. But avoid sarcasm or making a student the butt of a joke. Keep the humor positive. A number of teachers have been successful by acting things out like wearing costumes. If you are comfortable, try it.

74 | **Make Learning Visual.** As a result of television, video games, and movies, the students that we teach are more visual learners than ever before. Put posters, student drawings, and student work showing successful models around the room. Show positive graphs. Don't show negative things like failures on a test. Show the improved (hopefully) number of students who are passing. You do not have to show test scores.

If you want to get posters, consider writing to government agencies like NASA, or to airplane companies like Boeing or Delta Airlines. Go to a local movie theater or to a video rental store like Blockbuster or Hollywood Video and ask for movie posters.

75 | **Celebrate Student Success.** If the class does well on a test, complement students on their accomplishments. You might also consider skipping giving homework on that day to show your appreciation of students doing well.

76 | **Remind Students Why They Are in School.** Kids love money. Don't we all. But students do not see the value of education for its own sake. We need to remind them that education will help them achieve many things, but for them, money might be primary. "How many of you want to make a million dollars? Stay in school and graduate. That is how much your high school diploma is worth. How many of you would like to make $4 million? That is what a college diploma is worth today.

77 | **Be on the Look Out for CPAs (Constant Pains in the ... Neck).** There are a few students who will seek to upset you and the learning environment of the class. They know exactly what buttons to push. Remain positive. Handle discipline problems in your "office" (right outside the door of the classroom.) Have the student with their back to the classroom so that you can watch the class.

78 **The Job of a Teacher.** The job of a teacher is to balance the difficult with the impossible. You need to be friendly with your charges yet remain aloof enough to be respected. You need to be steadfast yet flexible; consistent yet stretchy; warm and friendly yet distant. Sounds like an impossible task? Don't worry; you're up to it.

79 **Remember You're Getting Older and They're Not.** There is a growing age gap between you and the students. We need to ask "What is the role of teaching?" How do you maintain your distance and at the same time serve as mentor, teacher, and friend?

80 **Call Me Old Fashioned.** Educators want to be treated as professional. Dress like a professional. Doctors do. Lawyers do. Accountants do. I have seen teachers who come to school in ripped jeans, shorts, and T-shirts with cutoff sleeves. Some teachers fall back on the argument that students do not have dress standards. Why should they? I know that there is a desire to relate to students, but there needs to be a gap between student behavior and teacher behavior.

81 | **Time to Take Temperature.** Ask students, "Do you understand what I am teaching?" Have students respond by giving thumbs up or thumbs down. Ask students whose thumbs are down what you can do to clarify the topic. Responses to the thumbs up/ thumbs down scenario can help you assess if you are meeting the students' needs.

82 | **Create Different Paths for Learning.** Most at-risk learners hate to memorize textbook facts. They are easily bored with that and frequently their behavior reflects that boredom; they act out and become disruptive. Find ways to engage them. We need to teach students how to think as well as what to think. We need to engage them in their own learning.

One of the best exercises I ever used when I was teaching economics dealt with supply and demand. One of the most boring things to teach (and learn) is supply and demand. I told my classes that I would give them a take home test and that they could start the test in class in groups but they had to write the answers at home. The test consisted of one question. The setup: "It is announced today, that eating a lemon a day will prevent you from getting cancer. What happens to the price, supply, and demand for lemons tomorrow? Next year? Five years from tomorrow?" Students became enthused about working out the answer. They turned to other students to help them arrive at some sort of response. Some of the brighter students pointed out that lemon production could not increase overnight or even next year because lemon trees took time to produce lemons. Some children handed in the results using graphs or charts. They became far more creative then I thought by using the Web to contact the Lemon Growers Association. They suggested hiring the best scientists to find ways of growing artificial lemons.

While the example above is for high school social studies teachers, I believe that you can develop similar lessons dealing with your subject areas.

83 | **Walk Around.** Besides being good for your health, walking around your classroom gives you an opportunity to see the students at work. It also gives students the opportunity to see you. Students who sit in the back will be able to hear you better. Avoid working behind a lectern or a desk, it isolates you from the students and at the same time creates the illusion that you are distant from the learning environment. Do not allow the classroom to establish artificial barriers between you and the students.

84 | **Document, Document, Document.** Keep records about your students. Document attendance, lateness, referrals, absences, visits to the dean's office. While it takes time, you will ultimately find out that you will save yourself a good deal of grief when called on to justify grades. Also, keep a record of phone calls and letters sent home to parents or guardians.

85 | **Tough Questions.** There are four major causes of students dropping out of school:

1. The child him/herself;
2. The family situation;
3. The community they live in; and
4. The school environment.

In order to prevent students from dropping out of school, we must attack the causes that are in our control. We cannot address the community they live in or, in most cases, their family situation. These are out of our control. But we can address the choices they make and the school environment. One of the ways of doing so is for educators to ask a serious, tough questions.

86 | **Creating an Inviting Classroom.** How inviting is the environment in your classroom? Are the walls painted in "happy colors" or are they a drab, institutional gray or green? Are your bulletin boards filled with student work, with commercial advertisements, or left blank?

87 | **Engaging Students.** Are *all* students encouraged to learn? Has the school created different classes for students—those designed to pass and those designed to fail? Those who will go on to college and those who will drop out? What role can you, as a classroom instructor, play in overcoming this paradigm?

How many of the students that start in your school or system graduate? Does the school track their progress through the system? Are "safety nets" built in for those who are identified as at-risk? What "pillars" support these safety nets? Are you one of these safety nets? Do you know how to get additional assistance in helping students graduate? Is there additional counseling, mentoring, afterschool learning activities, or service-learning projects designed to connect schooling to the world of work? As you track, is the largest reason for kids leaving school, "miscellaneous"?

88 | **Push Outs.** How many students who drop-outs are actually pushed out? (Students who are told, by word or action, "I do not want you in my class" or "I don't need you in my school.") How close to graduation are students who dropout? Do they need one credit or 10? What has the school done to help them make up the credit? What role can you, as a classroom instructor, play in overcoming this situation? What is done to support the "psychological" dropout—the child who is physically in school but mentally is miles away. What role can you, as a classroom instructor, play in overcoming this situation?

89 | **Students Crave Attention.** "Students crave our attention, and they will usually do whatever it takes to get it." —Annette Breaux

Catch students doing good things. Many of the at-risk learners have self-image problems. Complement them by saying, "good answer" or "thank you" for helping, doing homework, or being prepared.

90 | **How Many of You Are Perfect?** "Children are not perfect. And neither are we. Teachers who expect perfect behavior from their students are being extremely unrealistic and are inviting profound disappointment." —Annette Breaux

If you make a mistake, can you admit it? Admitting you have made a mistake will make you more human in the eyes of your students. So admit it and get over it.

91 | **Put Yourself in the Shoes of an At-Risk Learner.** How would you feel if you had to spend 9 or 10 years in school, being retained, tracked into slow classes with other "dumb" students, suspended on occasion, suffering through failure after failure on test after test, and then to have high-school counselors talk down to you about graduation credit, college entrance requirements, and your poor attitude?

Traditional teaching and learning techniques do not work with nontraditional students. If we want to succeed with nontraditional (at-risk) students we must use nontraditional teaching and learning techniques.

What characterizes nontraditional learners?

1. Short attention span;
2. Disconnected;
3. Easily bored;
4. Visual learners;
5. Come from nontraditional homes;
6. Want stability in their lives; and
7. Enjoy playing "games."

How can you take advantage of these (and the other strengths you've identified) and build on them to increase the academic achievement of all students?

92 | **Sending Students Out of the Room.** If students are late, do not send them to the office to get a late pass. This causes them to miss even more of the class than they already have. Ask them to stay after class or ask them to speak to you at the door of the classroom to explain why they were late.

93 | **Classroom Cheating.** Prevent it. Tell students in advance, before it happens, what you do if your suspect it. There are many Web sites that help students with writing term papers. Check Wikipedia first if you suspect that a student has "lifted" a paper. Make students aware that you know about Web sites like Wikipedia.

94 | **When Students Get Bored, What Does it Look Like?** Boredom is listed by the Bill and Melinda Gates Foundation report, *The Silent Epidemic*, as the leading cause of students dropping out of school. Be aware of student's physical behavior and body language. Is a child with their head on a desk simply tired or are they bored? Is a student who is sleeping in class overworked or working after school? Find out by asking. Ignoring the problem will not make it go away and could make others copy the behavior.

Where do bored students sit? Changing their seats might result in a changed behavior.

95 | **Classroom Objectives.** Imagine going on vacation without knowing where you are going. Imagine a doctor performing surgery without an objective. Make your objectives clear. Do your students know what they are expected to learn from the lesson you are teaching? Do *you* know what you expecting students to learn from the lesson? Lessons must have a clear, *measurable* objective.

96 | **Conducting a Lecture.** Lecturing is the least effective method of instruction, yet it is the most often used. You do not learn how to swim by being lectured by an expert on swimming. Don't teach from the textbook. I took a college class with a professor who had participants sit on the workbook. He said, "Now you have covered the material. How many of you feel smarter?" The ineffective teacher uses the textbook to tell him what to teach, how to teach it, when to teach it and what questions to ask. No textbook has an exact correlation to the district's curriculum. That doesn't mean you cannot use the textbook. It means that the textbook is a tool. Be creative. Vary the lessons by using reenactments, lecture, role-playing, silent or aloud reading, reading to students, or conducting a question and answer session.

97 | **Give Graduates a Job.** I had a great geometry teacher. (I was not a great geometry student.) I asked her why we were learning the Pythagoras Theorem. She said, "If you ever want to measure the height of a pyramid and you know two sides, you can figure out what the measurement of the other side is. You can do it." I have never had to measure the height of a pyramid. Relevance is education's "4th R." Relate what you are teaching to real-life connections. Students (and you) need to see the relevance in the material you teach. You need to build a bridge between what you teach and what the students can relate to. Most students will understand things if you explain to them how this will help them in the future—in the job market or their future lives.

98 | **Give Students a Break.** Television has helped create a timed break every 12-19 minutes. Our students are used to that. Have students take stretch breaks. "When I say go, you have 45 seconds to stand up, stretch, and talk to your neighbors. When I say stop you must be seated and quiet." Or you can have them play three rounds of paper, rock, and scissors. It will give them a break and you can either take a break or look at the material you will teach next.

99 | **Support Children's Strengths.** It is easy to identify the weaknesses of at-risk learners. Most of us rarely identify their strengths. They are risk takers; learn in different ways than traditional learners. Frequently they are leaders. Many write poetry or draw. We need to take advantage of these skills in developing and teaching. Maybe some of them can be used as mentors to some of the weaker students in your class or in your school.

100 | **What Do You Do to Support Children Who Are At-Risk of Failure?** I once had a teacher tell me, "Franklin, I could be a much better teacher if I had better students." Couldn't we all. The students who need us the most sometimes get teachers who ignore them or treat them unfairly. We need to support all students, not just the brightest. Parents are not holding their better children at home waiting for the system to improve. Imagine you were the parent of a weak student. How would you feel if you felt that your child was not getting the proper respect or treatment because they weren't "a better student?"

101 | **Never Forget What You Do.** Have you ever been engaged in a dinner conversation with a stranger or with a group of friends, or members of your family who ask, "What do you do for a living?" And when you reply, "I am an educator," they look at you as if you have two heads. "You have it easy. You only work 180 days a year and only work 6 hours a day." If this has ever happened to you, why don't you copy the story below and give them a copy?

The dinner guests were sitting around the table discussing life.

One man, a CEO, decided to explain the problem with education. He argued, "What's a kid going to learn from someone who decided his best option in life was to become a teacher?" He reminded the other dinner guests what they say about teachers: "Those who can, do. Those who can't, teach." To stress his point he said to another guest; "You're a teacher, Bonnie. Be honest. What do you make?"

Bonnie, who had a reputation for honesty and frankness replied, "You want to know what I make …? She paused for a second, then began, "Well, I make kids work harder than they ever thought they could. I make a C+ feel like the Medal of Honor. I make kids sit through 40 minutes of class time when their parents can't make them sit for 5 without an I Pod, Game Cube, or movie rental. You want to know what I make?" She paused again and looked at each and every person at the table. "I make kids wonder. I make them question. I make them apologize and mean it. I make them have respect and take responsibility for their actions. I teach them to write and then I make them write. Keyboarding isn't everything. I make them read, read, read. I make them show all their work in math. They use their God given brain, not the man-made calculator. I make my students from other countries learn everything they need to know in English while preserving their unique cultural identity. I make my classroom a place where all my students feel safe. I make my students stand, placing their hand over their heart to say the Pledge of Allegiance to the Flag, One Nation Under God, because we live in the United States of America. I make them understand that if they use the gifts they were given, work hard, and follow their hearts, they can succeed in life." Bonnie paused one last time and then continued. "Then, when people try to judge me by what I make, with me knowing money isn't everything, I can hold my head up high and pay no attention because they are ignorant…. You want to know what I make? I MAKE A DIFFERENCE. What do you make Mr. CEO?"

Family and Community Involvement

All parents, regardless of their race, ethnicity or economic background, want their children to do well in school. Parents need to be involved with school and not just to collect money or to serve as volunteers. Educators know the data that parent involvement falls off as children go through the educational process. More parents are involved with their children's education in elementary school than in middle and high school. Yet children's needs increase as they age. The pressure of peers, the demands of growing up, the "call" of drugs, alcohol, and gangs all cause young people to consider dropping out of school. Schools cannot do the job of education without parent and family involvement. The question then becomes one of how to get parents involved.

102 | **Communicate With Parents.** The electronic age has provided schools with additional means of contacting parents. Teachers can "correspond" to parents via e-mail. Teachers should set up an e-mail address using either, MSN, AOL, Yahoo, or Gmail. That account, rather than your personal account, should be given to parents at meetings or sent home with students. Write a weekly or monthly newsletter. The newsletter need not be long or involved but merely an attempt to keep parents abreast of their children's learning.

Have students write a newsletter to parents to take some of the burden and responsibility off of your shoulders. Find out if the employers of your students' parents will allow you to send e-mails to their places of work. If your school has a Web site, post homework assignments on the site.

103 | **Student-Led Parent Conferences.** Invite students to attend student-parent conferences. You may need to train them so that they can lead these conferences. The advantage of having students available is that the meeting may be less confrontational as they have to explain poor grades, unexcused absences, lateness, and truancy.

Allow your students to choose what they want their parents to see.

Keep a folder of student work to show parents. Clearly state to the parent or guardian what are the expectations of the class and child. Prepare a sheet with the expectations clearly spelled out (homework, tests, classwork, discipline.)

Do not make meetings personal. Act professionally. A small number of parents will try to upset you and become defensive, defending their child's behavior. It may be that they have had so many negative reports about their child that they may be overwhelmed and not know how to address their concerns. Control your reactions. Think about what you want to say before you say it.

When contacting a parent about their child's behavior, prepare a script of what you plan to say. Have documentation (date, time, infraction)

104 | **The Parents of Dropouts.** Data indicate that children who dropout of school sometimes have parents who have dropped out of school. Coming to school for a meeting may be intimidating to parents. See if the principal is willing to set up parent meetings off-campus, possibly at a community center or a church where parents would feel more at home.

105 | Parental Involvement. Ask parents to become more involved with your class or school by:

- Mentoring a child;
- On a Career Day, having them explain to children what their work entails;
- Volunteering to have a low-performing child read to them; or
- Serving on a school committee.

106 | Sign Parent Contracts. Parents have signed contracts with a variety of businesses. They understand that a contract is an agreement with two or more parties, spelling out the obligations of each to the other. Why shouldn't schools use contracts to spell out the obligations of the school to them and spell out what is expected of them. Have the parents' association help you frame the contract.

At one of the schools where I worked, I developed a parent contract spelling out what was expected from parents and what they could expect from the school.

I, as the parent or guardian of _____ agree to the following conditions:

1. I pledge to attend at least 6 of the 10 parent's association meetings. These meetings are held the first Tuesday of every month beginning at 6 P.M.

2. I pledge that I will regularly check my child's homework.
3. I pledge that I will regularly check my child's tests.
4. I pledge that I will check my child's report card when issued, six times a year on or about the following dates: _____, _____, _____, _____, _____, _____.
5. I pledge that my child will get a good night's sleep.
6. I pledge that my child will arrive at school on time.
7. I pledge that my child will have a place at home to study.
8. I pledge that I will help my child with homework (when I can.)
9. I pledge that I will talk about school with my child at least twice a week.
10. I pledge that I will read with my child.
11. I pledge that I will talk to my child's teachers on Open School Day. This year Open School Day will be held _____.
12. I will contact the school if my child is unable to attend because of illness or family emergencies.

_____   _____
Parent or Guardian's Name   Telephone # at home

_____   _____
Name of Student   Telephone # at work

_____
Address

_____   _____
E-mail   Cell phone

In return, the school has the following obligations to you:

1. The school will regularly contact you regarding your child's academic achievement by report card, Open School Nights, letters home, and e-mails.
2. The school will post on its Web site, www._____ your child's homework, school curriculum, student handbook and _____.
3. Your child's teacher(s) will contact you if your child is late, or absent, or misbehaves.
4. In the event that school is closed, the Web site will have all information concerning school holidays or teacher training days.

Add to this list whatever items are necessary to meet the needs of your individual school. Distribute this form to parents in person (at meetings, school events like plays or sporting events), by e-mail, by sending it home with children, or by mail.

107

Conduct Surveys of Parents of At-Risk Students. Many of the parents of at-risk learners have had negative school experiences themselves. It would be of great use if we had certain information about how they address learning issues with their child/children. Many parents envision their own, possibly negative, school experiences before coming to school meetings. Data show that at-risk students frequently come from homes where parents were at-risk themselves. We need to make schools and classrooms welcoming and parent-friendly.

108

A Clean Classroom Gives the Right Impression. Have the custodian clean your room before a parent meeting. Make sure that your desk is clean and uncluttered. Make sure that the blackboard is clean and that the chalk dust has been removed. Parents will take notice. Nobody wants to visit a home that is uninviting, so treat your classroom as if it were your home. Think about it, many of you spend more waking hours there than you do at home.

109 | **Use Family's First Language When Conducting Interviews.** Have you ever gone to a foreign country and been uncomfortable when someone spoke in his or her native language and you didn't understand what was being said? Parents may not be comfortable conducting an interview in English. One of the first questions to be asked before beginning an interview, is "Are you uncomfortable conducting this interview in English?" If the response is in the affirmative, get a translator. School secretaries who answer the telephone should ask the same question when answering the outside telephone. A bilingual parent may be recruited to translate or use one of your better students. Have student translators available for parents who prefer speaking in a language other than English. We used our better academic students (National Honor Society students) to serve as translators.

110 | **Different Languages, Different Customs.** Extend your hand in friendship when parents come to visit. Understand that many of your parents will have different customs as well as different languages. In some societies, looking people in the eyes is a sign of disrespect. Being offered the left hand to shake is a sign of disrespect in some cultures. We need to be compassionate and show feelings of respect for their customs and traditions.

Another opportunity exists when papers are sent home to parents and they are in English. If announcements such as parent meetings are in English and the parents cannot read them, parents may not attend because they didn't understand the purpose of the note. When a large percentage of the school's population speaks one or more foreign languages then every opportunity should be made to reach parents in their native language.

111 | **Start on a Positive Note.** Start the interview on a positive note. Thank the parent for coming. Indicate that you know that they may have other things to do other than visiting schools. Do not only have negative things to say. Make positive phone calls to parents. Tell parents and complement them for their children's punctuality to class, for being well prepared, or that their child did well on an examination or at a sporting or school event.

112 | **Student Models.** Hang student work in your classroom. Parents and students need a replicable model of what "quality work" looks like. Create a template by having student work hanging in classrooms and the hall outside your room.

113 | **"We Don't Want To Brag" Bulletin Board, Part II.** Put positive news on a bulletin board that parents can notice when they enter the classroom. The work can include positive news about recent graduates, or some students who participated in out-of school events or their achieving degrees. Newspaper articles about the success of students in contests, sports, or achievements can be included. Include information or letters from graduates who are in college, the workforce, or the military.

114 | **Hang Graphs of Student Achievements.** Graphs showing improvements in testing or attendance can be placed in visible locations in the classroom. The graph lines should be going up not down. Graphs should emphasize the positive, not the negative. For example, show the number of students who passed your last test (but not the number of those who failed).

115 | **Celebrate Student Success.** Find occasions to celebrate the success of students whether in academics, sports, or student activities. Make sure to invite parents. Take "instant" pictures of parents celebrating with their children. The success should not create "winners" and "losers." Insure that every student can be a winner.

116
Send a Party Invitation Inviting Parents to Come to Meetings. Many communities have "dollar stores" where you can buy inexpensive invitations. Try inviting parents to school meetings. Depending on the age of your students, have them fill out the addresses of their parents. Their involvement makes the invitation more appealing. If the school doesn't have the postage available, consider sending the invitations home with the children.

117
Survey Parents to Determine What Topics They Want Addressed at Meetings. Schools generally set the agenda for parent meetings. When parents don't show up the assumption is that they are not interested in their children. We asked the parents what they wanted the meeting topics to be. They told us quite firmly that they didn't want us to discuss how to raise their children. They said that was their responsibility. What they did want was to learn about how to get their child into college, how to pay for college, and what opportunities existed after graduation for employment. We contacted a number of universities and had them send in representatives (which they were glad to do) to explain what courses the children needed to take. Another college sent in a financial aide officer to explain the various grants and loans available to students. The head of counseling office used books like *The Occupation Outlook Handbook* to explain what jobs were available to students for the next 10 years. In addition, they explained what were the requirements to take that job. While this

may have been unique to our school, it makes sense to ask the parents what their needs are and not assume that educators have the answers before any questions are asked.

118 | **Survey Parents to Determine What Times Are Best for Meetings.** The time and place may be inconvenient because they have other things that must be taken care of. Many parents work at night and so nighttime meetings may not work. They need to take care of younger children. Or their children may have other needs that must be addressed (i.e., Boy Scout meetings, Little League, etc.).

119 | **Develop Contact Information Including E-Mail and Cell Phone Information.** Whenever you meet with a parent have them fill out a new contact card. Many of our families move, change their telephone numbers, or e-mail. Keep a form available so that parents can fill them out. The question, "Do I have your current information available?" should be among the first questions you ask when parents visit.

120 | **Parent Homework Assignments.** The job of schools and teachers has increased so much that we need all the help we can get. Give parents "homework assignments" to ensure that they are helping their child. Have them mail it back to you so you can verify. This helps to keep a continual open line of communication.

121 | **"Welcome" Signs in a Variety of Languages.** By using Google you can find out how to say hello in a number of languages. Post them on or above your classroom door. In addition, post your name above the door and the subject(s) you teach.

122 | **Invite Parents to Sit in on Classes.** Depending on your comfort level, invite parents to visit class when you are teaching. Many parents are anxious to see their child learning some activity. Also identify parents' skills, hobbies, or occupations. You might want to invite them in and have them serve as a guest speaker.

123 | **Think About Sending Homework Home for Parents to Help With.** Teachers frequently give homework and suggest that students have their parents help them with it. We need to understand that there is a correlation between children at-risk and parents who have dropped out of school. In addition, single parents are today's norm. We have many parents who are working extra jobs and may not have the time or are too exhausted to help. Many parents are embarrassed when asked to help their child with homework. They may never have taken calculus or know anything about DNA. Think about asking children to ask parents to help with homework. It may leave a bad taste in the parent's mind about their own experience in school.

124 | **When Tragedy Strikes.** If a death or tragedy affects a family, send a condolence card or "get well card" or make a phone call. Is there an early alert system to identify those children who are going through trauma in their personal lives like divorce of parents, merging of families, incarceration of a family member, death of a member of the family? Do mechanisms exist to support the child who does not fit the traditional school mold (i.e., gay or lesbian children, nerds or geeks, ESL or special education students), or are they merely shunted off to alternative schools?

125 **Feed Them and They Will Come.** Nothing makes people feel more at home than food. When we held parent meetings we supplied food. How can schools obtain food for these meetings? The first obvious place is the school cafeteria. But other places might be willing to supply snacks. Try local fast food places. Tell the manager that you will supply thank you letters as well as publicize the store making the donation. Food can be obtained frequently free from supermarkets. If your school has an active parents association, parents can take turns bringing food to school.

126 **Give Away "Free Things."** See if you can get free tickets for parents to attend school events like plays, sports, or mock trials. If you attend a conference, see if you can get free pens or pencils or other doodads that you can distribute to parents who attend meetings.

127 **Make Positive Phone Calls to Parents.** Call parents early in the year, with positive news. Most phone calls made to homes tend to be negative. Usually when the parent of an at-risk child gets a phone call, the first reaction is "what did he do now?" Parents who get positive phone calls appreciate it. Find something about the child that is positive. "He brought his notebook today." "She came on time." Positive feedback can change parent's attitudes about what they expect to hear from teachers. If a student complains about the phone call ("Why did you call my house?"), explain to them that you always work with parents in their best interests. Make clear that you make both positive and negative phone calls home. The word will get out to other students.

128 | **Everyone Bring One.** One of the most successful programs we instituted at our school was "Everyone Bring One." We asked parents to attend our parent meetings and to bring someone with them to the meeting, preferably another parent. In order to encourage their attendance, we gave each attendee a "strip lottery ticket." If they brought one person, they received two lottery tickets, one for themselves and one for their guest. The guest also received a lottery ticket. If they brought 10 people, they received 11 tickets, one for them and one for each of their guests. At the end of the meeting we drew for prizes. Our prizes consisted of "buy one, get one for free" donated by local fast-food stores. Local merchants donated discontinued products such as radios. Big box stores (like Costco, and Sam's Club) made donations in return for publicizing that they made the donation. If the school has available monies, it might make multiple purchases of inexpensive alarm clocks sending a message that it is important for students to be on time.

129 | Use the Community to Make Announcements of Parent Meetings.

We asked priests, ministers, and rabbis to announce when we were holding parent meetings. In addition, we asked local supermarkets to post parent meeting schedules on their community bulletin boards. There was willingness for the community people to aid the school.

130 | Student Mentors.

If you have a community college, 4-year college, or university in your community, invite students from these institutions to teach your class. They have the ability to make links between principles and practice. By bringing in some projects they are working on, college students can link math, science, and history to the practical applications of material taught. There are other advantages as well.

Because of their age, they may have the ability to better relate to students. They may have the ability to speak a variety of foreign language. Some may have come from the same economic, social, or religious background that some of your students come from. Many college students also believe they have an obligation to help others.

In rural areas, they provide additional support to teachers and curriculum. They can answer questions that classroom educators may not have current information on, such as obtaining scholarships, money, and how to get an education in college.

131 **Technology "Burial Ground."** What do businesses do with their "old computers" and cash registers? We asked them to donate them to the school. If you have contacts within your own community or the community where the school is, ask the businesses to donate their used equipment to the school. We used old cash registers to teach math to our special education students. Elementary schools can use cash registers for the same purpose. You can teach simple mathematics or more complex math (percentages when adding tax for each purchase). The children might not understand the complexity of math but they do understand it when put in terms of dollars and cents.

If you are teaching in a pre school or elementary school, you might ask a business to donate "used paper" to school. Computer paper is only used on one side. Why not use the other side of the paper for drawing?

132 **Who Profits From Your School?** The business community is a major beneficiary from a high performing classroom, school and district. If you can find available time, see if you can join and speak to your chamber of commerce, the Rotary or other civic organizations. Do not go simply with hat in hand, but explain to them what they can do to help you help them.

133 | **A School Business Plan.** Schools need to develop all sorts of plans. They have school safety plans, instructional plans, strategic plans, and so on. I believe that every school and teacher needs to have a business plan. Supposing you met a business person who said to you, "I want to help the school or your class, what do you suggest that I do?" How would you respond? Would you stutter or would you have some idea of what would benefit your students?

134 | **Open Lines of Communication.** Most states fund their schools using property taxes. As the population ages, it becomes increasingly critical that members of the community see a value in their schools. If you are a member of a community group, meet with representatives of the community including church leaders, and community-based organizations like the Chamber of Commerce, Rotary, Lions, etc. Have them announce school events like parent meetings, sporting events, student performances. See if you can give them tickets to school sporting events and student performances.

135 | **Local Business People.** If you frequent neighborhood businesses, ask these business people to come to your classroom and serve as "experts" in their business field, explaining their background, whether they had to attend college in order to enter the field, why it is important to finish school, and so on. This helps build good will as well as showing a different perspective that you might not have.

136 | **Local Residents.** Some residents have real-life experiences that will add depth to class discussions. Some might be war veterans, retired scientists, or engineers. Using their experiences adds a first-hand source to what you are teaching. It becomes a win-win situation. Students win with primary source information. You win because you are adding depth. They win, because the residents pay for schools with tax money, vote on school budgets, and can see how their money is being spent.

Safe Schools

School violence is nothing new. In the 1960s a film titled, *The Blackboard Jungle* depicted violence in an inner-city school. But the violence in West Paducah, Kentucky, Columbine, Colorado and an Amish community shows that crime has spiraled out of the inner city to rural and suburban America. The violence level has increased to include handguns and automatic weapons. The FBI's "School Shooter Report" states that 161,000 students do not come to school each day because they are afraid. If they do not come to school, they do not learn. If they do not learn, they are at-risk. If they are at-risk, then they may dropout.

137 | **Preventing School Violence.** Students, parents, and staff deserve a safe environment where learning can take place. The shooting at Columbine High School in Littleton, Colorado, in April 1999, shocked the country. As the Federal Bureau of Investigation has written in its report, *The School Shooter: A Threat Assessment Perspective*, "Adolescent violence in general, and homicides in particular, have decreased since 1993, but that hopeful trend has been somewhat obscured in the nationwide wave of concern over school shootings. This recent form of adolescent violence is in fact quite rare. But the sudden, senseless deaths of teenagers and teachers in the middle of a school day, for no comprehensible reason, is far more shocking and gets far more attention than the less extreme acts of violence that happen in schools every week. Under the intense spotlight of national media coverage, a tragedy such as the Columbine High School shooting spreads horror, shock, and fear to every corner of the country. Educators, mental health professionals, legislators, law enforcement officers, parents, students, and the rest of the public all share a sense of frustration and helplessness and a compulsion to take some quick action that can prevent similar incidents in the future."

What can schools do to prevent such incidents from happening? I have worked in some violent schools as well as schools which should be seemingly immune to school violence. In one affluent, college-oriented school that I worked in, a student was shot and killed in the schoolyard. For the next few weeks, the school was the focus of media attention. I formed what we called "the crisis council" to prevent further violence on the school campus. We organized a class of freshmen, sophomores, juniors, and seniors. The group met once a month or more frequently, if necessary. The students were served milk, juice, and snacks. The most difficult part was convincing the students that it was their school as much as it was the staffs', and that any violence that took place on campus would be damaging to their careers, college chances, employment, and so forth. I, representing the school, wanted to know, in advance, if they knew if any violence or illegal activity was going to take place in or around the school. There would be absolute confidentiality unless the reported incident was going to be of danger to a group of students or to themselves.

There was a need to develop trust in this group, another hurdle. But as a result, suicides were prevented, illegal substances were snatched before they could be put to use, and reports of gang activity were reported to the police department.

138 | What Classroom Teachers Can Do.
What can classroom teachers do to prevent violence? First, and most importantly, be aware of what is happening around you and be available and open to your students. Insure confidentiality if a student tells you something as long as it doesn't hurt them (i.e., suicide) or doesn't hurt someone else. Students need someone they can trust and believe in, just as they expect that you will believe in them.

139 | **Every School Should Have a COSA.** The Board of Education of the City of New York created a high school position called the Coordinator of Student Activities. I was privileged to have been selected to serve in that position. Of all the jobs I had in education, it was my favorite. In addition to coordinating all student activities, we taught classes and served as "a third ear" for students. Counselors in schools are too often overburdened by paperwork, programming, and other tasks not related to counseling. Student government officials represent the really good students. Members of teams and clubs have coaches and faculty advisors to confide in. By COSAs taking it upon themselves to listen to children who lacked a voice in school we hoped to prevent untoward incidents like fights, riots, and drug use. Students knew they could speak to a COSA with total anonymity with two exceptions. One, the information would not cause harm to the student reporting the incident. (We didn't want to know if the student was going to commit suicide and we would be bound to not reporting it.) The second condition was if the information would cause harm to others (i.e., fights, riots, etc.) Many fights and gang incidents were prevented by the actions of COSAs. COSAs saw the job of listening to students who frequently lacked any adult who listened to them. Every student in every school should feel that he or she has a trusting relationship with at least one adult in the school. Imagine the impact if every teacher were to "adopt" by listening to at least one student in each class.

140 | **Sanctuaries of Safety.** Before schools can become citadels of learning they need to be sanctuaries of safety. The FBI in its *School Shooters Report* says that 161,000 students do not come to school because they are afraid. Gallop Polls indicate that "lack of discipline" is one of the most serious problem facing America's schools. What can classroom teachers do? First, there needs to be a realization that learning can only take place in safe, orderly, well-managed classrooms. There needs to be clear and broad-based rules with clearly stated consequences for breaking those rules. Classroom teachers should have students input into the development of no more than seven rules. If students are involved in the development of those rules, they are more likely to have ownership. Teachers should ensure that those rules are consistently enforced. Nothing is as disheartening to students to see that some students have to live by the rules while others are exempt. The easiest way of enforcement is to have students internalize the rules by self-discipline and positive peer pressure. Teachers need to recognize positive classroom behavior (which should be the norm) by individuals and the class. If students perform extraordinary acts of selflessness, then there needs to be contact made with their parents and guardians.

Do not:

- Make vague rules that are open to a variety of interpretation;
- Make rules that are difficult or impossible for you to enforce;
- Make rules that contradict school or district policy;

- Lose your temper when enforcing rules;
- Respond inconsistently to student misbehavior;
- Make decisions where the punishment exceeds the infraction;
- Use physical or public punishment; or
- Use sarcasm or ridicule.

Do:

- Provide students with opportunities to be successful; and
- Teach students to monitor their own behavior.

141

Bullying. The prevention of bullying has become a hot-button issue in many schools. The FBI, in its *School Shooter Report* (www.fbi.gov), says that 161,000 children a day do not come to school because they are afraid. Research has indicated that teachers can no longer treat bullying as a normal growing up occurrence. What can classroom educators do to prevent bullying?

142 | **What You Can Do About Bullying.** Treat bullying seriously. Remember Smokey the Bear's advice, "It is easier to prevent, then to put out." You need to create a classroom climate that builds trust and respect for all, and establishes that bullying is unacceptable. When you have to react, react quickly and decisively.

Do not look the other way when incidents involving bullying occur. Bullying may be a physical act but also may be a verbal act. Treat them both as equally serious. Take immediate action when bullying is observed. All teachers and school staff must let children know they care and will not allow anyone to be mistreated. By taking immediate action and dealing directly with the bully, adults support both the victim and the witnesses.

Confront bullies in private. Challenging bullies in front of their peers may actually enhance their status and lead to further aggression. Refer both victims and aggressors to counseling when appropriate. Provide protection for bullying victims when necessary. Such protection may include creating a buddy system whereby students have a particular friend or older buddy on whom they can depend and with whom they share class schedule information and plans for the school day.

143 | **Bullying—Involve Your Students.** We need to provide students with opportunities to talk about bullying, and enlist their support in recognizing bullying as unacceptable behavior. Involve students in establishing classroom rules against bullying. Depending on the grade level, we need to develop classroom activities and discussions related to bullying and violence—including the harm that it causes—and develop strategies to reduce their incidence. Develop a classroom action plan to ensure that students know what to do when they observe a bully-victim confrontation. Teach cooperation by assigning projects that require collaboration. Such cooperation teaches students how to compromise and how to assert without demanding. Take care to vary group participants and to monitor the treatment of and by participants in each group.

144 | **Bullying—Involve Parents.** Notify parents of both victims and bullies when a confrontation occurs, and seek to resolve the problem expeditiously at school. Listen receptively to parents who report bullying, and investigate reported circumstances so immediate and appropriate school action may be taken.

Avoid attempts to mediate a bullying situation. The difference in power between victims and bullies may cause victims to feel further victimized by the process or to believe they are somehow at fault.

Other issues include:

♦ Be aware that bullying contributes to low self-esteem, depression, lower attendance rates, and higher rates of crime.
♦ If you suspect abuse, report it to your supervisor.
♦ Keep a journal of untoward incidents.
♦ If you suspect a student may be suicidal, do you know what do you do?
♦ Let students know from the beginning that "bad language" will not be tolerated. Part of bad language is racial or religious slurs.
♦ What do you do to insure that you have a safe classroom?
♦ For your own safety, do not have meetings at night or early in the day when you are alone in the building.

145 | Things Teachers Should Never Do.

♦ Never turn your back on the class when engaged in a one-on-one conversation.
♦ Never touch a student.
♦ Never argue with a student.
♦ Never embarrass a student in front of the class.
♦ Never stay in a classroom alone with a student behind closed doors.
♦ Never, never strike a student or aggressively grab a student.

- If you do, notify a supervisor of the incident as soon as possible.
- Avoid using threats, especially when you cannot enforce them.
- Avoid leaving the classroom.

146 | **Classroom Discipline.** We all have had the experience of a youngster who disrupts instruction. Each of us deals with it in our own way.

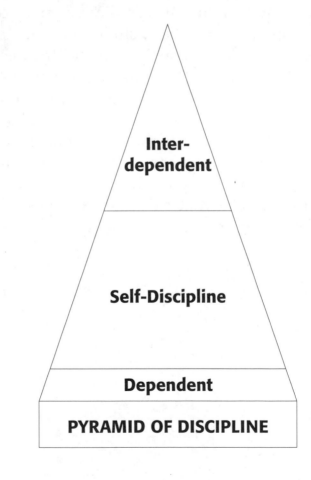

Inter-
dependent

Self-Discipline

Dependent

PYRAMID OF DISCIPLINE

Most of the current discipline we use in classrooms is what I call dependent discipline. It is dependent on the discipliner not the disciplinee. It is based on the idea of, "do what I say or I will hurt you. I will fail you. I will suspend or expel you. I will remove you from this class." Students have seen or experienced so much violence in their lives that they have become immune to any form or external punishment or discipline.

Many researchers feel that self-discipline is the approach we should use, but I believe that many students cannot control their own behavior.

I believe that what we should look at is what I call interdependent discipline. It is predicated on the concept of positive peer pressure. Many students are accustomed to peer pressure. Unfortunately, much of the peer pressure is negative. In order to succeed with interdependent discipline we need to teach students that a disruptive student is not only harmful to you as a teacher, but to the instruction of the class and to the reputation of the school as well. I believe and have seen that most students want to learn and once taught about positive discipline approaches will take your side and exert positive pressure on the disruptor.

147

What Do You Do in a Fight? Violence has come to pervade our society. It is visible on our televisions, in our movies, in our workplace, on tape, on CDs, in video games, and in sports. The violence that pervades our society also pervades the public school system. Conflict is a part of daily life in our culture. Only, too often, conflict is seen as a problem that needs to be eliminated or removed, rather than a situation that can be worked through and used constructively. Faced with problems, young people often resort to confrontation (lashing out) or avoidance (suppressing anger and fear). These responses, though natural, are inappropriate and can be harmful in the long run.

If you see a fight, do not put yourself in the middle of it. If you see a trusted student, send them to an office (the principal, assistant principal, security, or dean) to get help.

Maintain your cool. Do not overreact. Remain calm. Take several deep breaths. Think of what you will say and do in the event of a fight. A cool, rational approach will do more than someone who is screaming at the top of their lungs for the combatants to stop. Do not threaten as this will only inflame the fighters.

If you recognize any of the students involved in the fight, use their name and tell them to stop fighting. ("Jimmy, stop fighting!") The minute someone has stopped fighting you will find it easier to stop the fight.

The easiest way to stop a fight is to prevent it from happening in the first place.

Teachers need to teach students the downside of fighting. Young people must learn that disagreements are inevitable and that eliminating conflict is not a realistic goal. They need to learn how to de-escalate conflict, manage it, and resolve it. All schools, at all grade levels, should teach violence prevention and conflict resolution. Conflict-resolution skills begin with simple measures—active listening, effective communication without blaming or accusing, brainstorming nonviolent solutions—and extend to diversity awareness and empathy for the feelings of others. Conflict resolution seeks a solution that is satisfactory to both parties. The focus is taken away from the problem and the person and placed squarely on the solution. This strategy works well after anger has been diffused.

Teachers that implement a comprehensive program for violence prevention and conflict resolution must act on many fronts. School personnel must look for the early warning signs of aggression and violence, then devise interventions that halt its growth. Early intervention programs can teach students how to be aware of and overcome the violence that surrounds and influences them. Children of preschool and kindergarten age can learn the conflict-resolution skills of empathy, impulse control, and managing anger. Such programs, implemented in preschool and/or elementary school, teach nonviolent behavior, a life skill that will continue to develop in the later years of adolescence and adulthood.

A conflict-resolution program introduced at the pre-K level, can be used year after year, and rise with those students through the school system until children of all ages, at all grade levels, are resolving their conflicts constructively. The skills of conflict resolution spread through the school district and spill over into home and family life. Eventually, the entire community reaps the benefits.

148 | Preventing Suicide.

Preventing Suicide. Suicide is the third leading cause of teenage death in the United States. Suicide deaths remain high in the 15 to 24 age group with 3,971 suicides in 2001 and over 132,000 suicide attempts in 2002. In 1996, more teenagers and young people died of suicide than from cancer, heart disease, AIDS, birth defects, stroke, pneumonia and influenza, and chronic lung disease *combined*. If we would like to prevent it we need to recognize the symptoms. Some common symptoms of these disorders include:

- Extreme personality changes;
- Loss of interest in activities that used to be enjoyable;
- Significant loss or gain in appetite;
- Difficulty falling asleep or wanting to sleep all day;
- Fatigue or loss of energy;
- Feelings of worthlessness or guilt;
- Withdrawal from family and friends;
- Neglect of personal appearance or hygiene;
- Sadness, irritability, or indifference;
- Having trouble concentrating;
- Extreme anxiety or panic;
- Drug or alcohol use or abuse;
- Aggressive, destructive, or defiant behavior;
- Poor school performance; and
- Hallucinations or unusual beliefs.

149

What Can You Do About Suicide? Recognize that you (and I) are not experts about suicide nor have we been trained in dealing with it. If you see any of the signs listed in item 148, contact people in the school who are more knowledgeable and better trained to deal with the situation. These include: counselors, social workers, psychologists, the school nurse, and your principal.

150

In-School Suspension. According to an article in the *Milwaukee Journal Sentinel* (2008), Nearly half of all ninth graders, for example, are suspended at least once a year, and many of those students are suspended multiple times.

When a student "cuts" class or "ditches" school entirely, what do we do? We punish them by saying you are suspended. Think about it. A student doesn't come to class or school and we say, "Your punishment is not coming to school." It doesn't make a lot of sense to me. If your school has an in-school suspension program, use it. Make sure it is not merely an attempt to take disruptive students out of classrooms or to give students a break from learning. Supply the in-school suspension teacher with work for the student to do and make sure he/she does it. The ways to insure that the work is done is grade it and return it to both the student and the parent.

If your school does not have an in-school suspension program, ask the principal to establish one. Sending a disruptive or ditching student home to watch television, play video games, or get into trouble outside of school doesn't sound like punishment to me.

151 | **Truancy.** Woody Allen has said, "90% of success is simply based on showing up." If students do not come to school, they cannot learn and if they do not learn they place themselves at risk. Truancy is a major contributor to student failure and dropping out. Identify a truant early by looking at the following warning signs:

1. Keep accurate records to spot students who are frequently absent. Keep a record of notes from parents excusing absences.
2. Notify parents/guardians about absences.
3. Keep track of when student was absent. Was it the day of a test or some other important work?
4. Enforce the district's attendance policy fairly and consistently.
5. It may sound foolish, but make sure parents and students know the starting time for school and your class. Notify students and parents at the beginning of the term of the guidelines for absences and consequences of excessive absences.
6. If a student is absent for 3 days, make sure those in charge are notified.
7. Direct students who have been absent due to a chronic illness to the school nurse for follow-up.
8. Request a conference with parents whose student exhibits chronic absenteeism to discuss and provide them with a record of the student's attendance.
9. Encourage a classroom climate that is cooperative, supportive, and democratic.
10. Make your classroom an exciting place to be. Reassure students that they have a safe, secure place in

the classroom and that you like having them there.

11. Develop incentives for student attendance on a daily, weekly, 6-week, and semester basis.

12. Plan special Monday and Friday activities as these days have been identified as the most likely to produce high absenteeism.

13. Impress upon students how important a record of regular attendance and dependability is to prospective employers.

14. Prominently display motivational posters, attendance graphs, and certificates of recognition for good attendance.

15. Explain to students (when applicable) the importance of attendance and its role in learning, to future employees, colleges, and so on.

16. Involve students in the formulation of class attendance policies and the consequences of infractions.

17. Discuss with students ways that truancy can be diminished (purchase an alarm clock).

18. Ask a student to call a classmate who has been absent to remind them to come to school the next day.

19. Pair a student with absentee problems with two students who attend school regularly. Reward the three when all are present.

152 **Why We Do What We Do.** Whenever the everyday burdens of the job get you down, whenever you get depressed, whenever a student, parent, or supervisor picks on you, whenever you forget why you became an educator, I need your to read this poem and remember.

The Bridge Builder
By Will Allen Dromgoogle
(1860–1934)

An old man, going a lone highway
Came at the evening, cold and gray,
To a chasm, vast and deep and wide,
Through which was flowing a sullen tide.
The old man crossed in the twilight dim
The sullen stream had no fears for him.
But it turned when safe on the other side
And built a bridge to span the tide.
"Old man," said a fellow pilgrim near,
"You are wasting strength with building here.
Your journey will end with the ending day
You will never cross the chasm, deep and wide—
Why build you the bridge at the eventide?"
The builder lifted his old gray head,
"Good friend, in the path I have come," he said
"There followeth after me today
A youth whose feet must pass this way
This chasm that has been naught to me,
To that fair-haired youth may a pit-fall be,
He too, must cross in the twilight dim
Good friend, I am building this bridge for him.

Resources

The following list of resources is not meant to be comprehensive nor are the listings intended as endorsements. I have found them to be helpful to me.

Books

Breaux, A. (2003). *101 "answers" for new teachers and their mentors*. Larchmont, NY: Eye on Education.

Blackburn, B. (2007). *Classroom instruction from A to Z*. Larchmont, NY: Eye on Education.

Borsuk, A. J. (2008, January 6). Suspension rate deemed too high: MSP superintendent seeks alternatives in minor matters. *Milwaukee Journal Sentinel*. Retrieved from http://www.jsonline.com/story/index.aspx?id= 704133

Bradley, D., Pauley, J., & Pauley, J. (2006). *Effective classroom management: Six keys to success*. Lanham, MD: Rowman & Littlefield Education.

Fleck, F. (2005) *What successful principals do! 169 tips for principals*. Larchmont, NY: Eye on Education.

Jones, F. (2000). *Tools for teaching*. Santa Cruz, CA: Fredric H. Jones & Associates.

Martin, K., & Brenny, K. (2005). *1000 best new teacher survival secrets*. Naperville, IL: Sourcebooks.

Rodgers, S., Ludington, J,. & Graham, S. (1999). *Motivation & learning*. Evergreen, CO: Peak Learning Systems.

Rodgers, S., & Graham, S. (2003). *The high performing toolbox: Succeeding with performance tasks, projects and assessments*. Evergreen, CO: Peak Learning Systems.

Rodgers, S., Ludington, J,. & Graf, B. (2003) *Teaching and training techniques*. Evergreen, CO: Peak Learning Systems.

Rominger, L., Laughrea, S. P., & Elkin, N. (2001). *Your first year as a high school teacher*. Roseville, CA: Prima.

Souther, B. (2008). *R + R + R = R + R + R, the R rules.* Highland, TX: Aha Press.

Thompson, J. (2007). *The first-year teacher's survival guide.* San Francisco: Jossey Bass.

Wong, H., & Wong, R. (2004). *The first days of school.* Mountain View, CA: Harry K. Wong Publications.

Wong, H., & Breaux, A. (2003). *New teacher induction: How to train, support, and retain new teachers.* Mountain View, CA: Harry K. Wong Publications.

U.S. Bureau of Labor Statistics. (Various years). *The occupation outlook handbook.* Washington, DC: Author.

> The *Occupational Outlook Handbook* is a nationally recognized source of career information, designed to provide valuable assistance to individuals making decisions about their future work lives. The handbook is revised every 2 years. For more information see, www.bls.gov/OCO/

Mind Game Books

Battaglia, P. (2002). *So you think you're smart: 150 fun and challenging brain teasers.* Charlotte, NC: Intl Puzzle Features

Bridgeland, J. M., DiIulio, J. J., Jr., & Morison, K. B. (2006, March). *The silent epidemic: Perspectives of high school dropouts* (A report by Civic Enterprises in association with Peter D. Hart Research Associates for the Bill and Melinda Gates Foundation). Washington, DC: Civic Enterprises.

Fernandez, J. J. M. (1996). *Quick to solve brainteasers.* New York: Sterling Press.

Fixx, J. (1978). *Solve it! A perplexing profusion of puzzles.* New York: Barnes and Noble Press.

Nelson, B. (1983). *101 brain teasers.* Phoenix, AZ: Kathy Kolbe Concept.

Phillips, L. (1985). *263 brain busters: Just how smart are you, anyway?* New York: Puffin.

Sloane, P. (1992). *Lateral thinking puzzlers*. New York: Sterling Press.

Srinivas, K. (2002). *Brain teasers.* Robert D. Reed

Sullivan, K., Cleary, M., & Sullivan, G. (2004). *Bullying in the secondary schools*. Thousand Oaks, CA: Corwin Press.

Weber, K. (1989). *Five-minute mysteries: 37 challenging cases of murder and mayhem for you to solve*. Philadelphia: Running Press Book.

Weber, K. (1996). *Even more five-minute mysteries: 40 new cases of murder and mayhem for you to solve*. Philadelphia: Running Press Book.

URLs

There are many fine educational Web sites out there. Here are just a few which I have found helpful.

http://store.apple.com/Catalog/US/Images/routingpage.html

♦ A number of computer companies will give educator discounts if you purchase a computer directly from them. Apple Computer has a link for educators. In addition, Apple has rebuilt, certified machines.

www.ed.gov

♦ This is the Web site for the U.S. Department of Education. From this Web site, you can obtain free information about a number of items and additional Web site resources.

http://www.educationworld.com

♦ This Web site lists resources under a variety of topics: lesson planning, professional development, technology integration, administrator's desk, school issues, more resources, early childhood, school notes, lifestyles, market place, lesson of the day.

http://www.stopbullyingnow.com
- ♦ Presents practical research-based strategies to reduce bullying in schools.

http://www.fbi.gov/publications/school/school2.pdf
- ♦ The School Shooter: A Threat Assessment Perspective

http://www.adaptivepath.com/blog/2007/09/04/checklist-for-speakers-getting-what-you-need-from-conference-organizers/
- ♦ Tips for speakers.

http://office.microsoft.com/en-us/clipart/default.aspx
- ♦ Free clipart.

http://images.google.com/imghp?hl=en&tab=wi
- ♦ Free clipart.

http://www.dial-a-teacher.com/index.html
- ♦ Online homework help.

www.woot.com
- ♦ Sells one item a day. Generally the product is electronic.

www.techbargains.com
- ♦ Dedicated to helping save money on technology product purchases and provides information on available rebates.

www.epinions.com
- ♦ People who have purchased products list their opinion of the value of the item. This may save you endless grief by buying a product that does not live up to what has been advertised.

http://ericir.syr.edu/Virtual/Lessons

- ◆ This collection contains more than 2,000 unique lesson plans which were written and submitted by teachers from all over the United States and the world. These lesson plans are also included in GEM, which links to over 40,000 online education resources.

www.edweek.com

- ◆ *Education Week* on the Web. Get the latest educational news.

www.ldonline.org

- ◆ LD OnLine claims to be the world's leading Web site on learning disabilities and ADHD, serving more than 200,000 parents, teachers, and other professionals each month.

www.lessonplanz.com

- ◆ LessonPlanz.com is searchable directory of free online lesson plans and lesson plan resources for all grades and subjects.

www.nea.org/helpfrom/growing/works4me/library.html

- ◆ Provides practical advice from classroom teachers distributed by the National Education Association, the largest teacher union in the country.

www.ocw.mit/edu/Ocwweb/hshome/home/index.htm

- ◆ This Massachusetts Institute of Technology site includes more than 2,600 video and audio clips from faculty lectures, as well as assignments and lecture notes. Some of the material is assembled on the site for specific high school classes, such as Advanced Placement biology, calculus, and physics, which are college-preparatory courses. The online portal also allows high school teachers to search by topic for faculty lectures and assignments and use them as they see fit.

www.proteacher.com

♦ A great resource for elementary school teachers.

http://www2.scholastic.com/browse/home.jsp

♦ A great resource of scholastic products for K-12 educators.

http://teachersnetwork.org

♦ Teachers Network is a nonprofit organization—by teachers, for teachers—dedicated to improving student learning in public schools nationally and internationally. Teachers Network uses the power of its Web site, for lesson plans, videos, and print resources.

www.teachertube.com

♦ TeacherTube provides an online community for sharing instructional videos. They seek to fill a need for a more educationally focused, safe venue for teachers, schools, and home learners. It is a site to provide anytime, anywhere professional development with teachers teaching teachers. It is a site where teachers can post videos designed for students to view in order to learn a concept or skill.

www.teachervision.com

♦ Excellent source for lesson plans. TeacherVision is a subscription-based service.

www.discoveryeducation.com

♦ A great resource for projects, lesson plans, etc.

http://puzzlemaker.discoveryeducation.com/

- ♦ Puzzlemaker is a puzzle generation tool for teachers, students, and parents. Create and print customized word search, criss-cross, math puzzles, and more using your own word lists.

www.free.ed.gov

- ♦ Another great resource including lesson plans, etc.

www.wikipedia.org

- ♦ A great resource for information. On the downside, the information may not be accurate and students may plagiarize if for papers.